Clockwise
advanced

Classbook

Amanda Jeffries

OXFORD
UNIVERSITY PRESS

Contents

01 NICE TO MEET YOU

In this lesson

- Look at starting and ending conversations.
- Practise making introductions.
- Focus on using different adjectives to agree with people.
- Practise asking questions tactfully.

Pronunciation

1 Look at the Tapescript on *p.110*. In pairs, predict the words with the main stress in each dialogue.

2 🔲3 Listen and check. Practise repeating after the tape.

3 In pairs, read the dialogues.

Speak for yourself

1 In which of these situations would you start a conversation with a stranger? How would you start the conversations?
- on a train / plane   • in a bar / café   • at a party   • at the cinema

2 Decide on three things you might ask when you meet someone for the first time.

3 In groups of three, introduce yourself and someone else at ...
- an informal party.   • a conference.

Listening
Starting and ending conversations

1 🔲1 Listen to eight conversation openers.
1 Say where each one might be taking place.
2 Predict what the response will be.

2 🔲2 Listen and check. What other responses are possible?

Vocabulary
Adjectives

> To agree with a critical statement, it is very common to use a synonym or an opposite adjective.
>
> 💬 This room's tiny.   💬 Yes, it's **very small**, isn't it?
>
> 💬 Yes, it isn't **very big**, is it?

1 Look at the adjectives in **A** and think of synonyms.

A		B	
tiny	tedious	sensible	warm
freezing	idiotic	considerate	nice
filthy	disgusting	interesting	clean
hideous	thoughtless	big	attractive

2 Now match the adjectives in **A** with their opposites in **B**.

3 In pairs, make exchanges using these prompts. Start with an adjective in **A** and respond with a synonym or an opposite.
- a meal   • the weather   • a film   • a car
- a hotel room   • a suggestion   • a friend / relative   • a building

English in use
Making introductions

Introducing yourself
Hello, I'm Anna. I work with a friend of Paul's.

Introducing other people
John, this is Tony. Tony, John.

Giving more information
We know each other from university.

1 [○4] Listen to six extracts. Note down two more examples for each of the categories above.

2 Which are more formal / informal? Which expressions did you use in *Speak for yourself*?

3 In groups of four, introduce yourself and other people formally and informally. Take it in turns to monitor the language used.

Asking questions tactfully

It is often more polite and tactful to avoid questions beginning with *Who*, *What*, *Where*, *How many*, etc., especially with someone you don't know very well.

You can ask *yes / no* questions instead, so that the other person can choose how much information to give.

Have you got the time? (not ~~What time is it?~~)

4 In pairs, ask and answer *yes / no* questions about these topics.
- last weekend
- your flat
- a holiday
- your English
- your family
- your job
- your ambitions
- travel

5 Match the sentences with one of the uses of *actually* in *Did you notice ...?*
1 Your face looks familiar but I don't think we've **actually** spoken.
2 'Have you got a moment?' 'I'm a bit busy, **actually**.'
3 'Where are you from, Australia?' 'No, New Zealand, **actually**.'
4 'I can't believe you **actually** met the Beatles.'
5 'What do you think of my haircut?' '**Actually**, I preferred it the way it was.'

Did you notice...?

⟲ We're old friends, **actually**.

Actually can be used in different ways.
- to soften something that is difficult to say
- to suggest that something is surprising
- to correct or contradict what someone has said
- to mean *in fact* or *in reality*
- to decline an offer or refuse more politely

Speak out

Imagine that you are at an international conference or a party.
- Move round the classroom starting conversations.
- Get to know as much about each person as you can.
- Introduce the person you have just met to someone else and pass on any information you have.

Remember
- Use a range of language for making introductions and being introduced.
- Use different conversation openers and endings.
- Use a range of adjectives for agreeing with people.
- Ask questions as tactfully as possible to find out information.

In this lesson

- Practise reading for detailed understanding.
- Study and practise words and expressions connected with time.
- Focus on how to describe trends.
- Talk about trends in your country.

Speak for yourself

1  Listen to three people describing the same problem. What is it? Which person do you most sympathize with?

2 Do you have enough time? What three things would you do if you had more time?

Reading

Detailed understanding

1 Before you read *The mad rush to save time*, predict three things the writer will discuss.

2 ⏱ **Against the clock!** You have four minutes to read the whole text and check your predictions.

THE MAD RUSH *TO SAVE TIME*

Time has become **a scarce commodity**. Everyone wants more of it. The refrain 'If only I had more time' echoes around offices and homes in the western world; 'hurry sickness' is becoming the malaise of the new millennium. All over the world, people are working longer and longer hours, and struggling to fit more and more into every day. Symptoms include jabbing the 'door close' button on lift doors to save the two to four seconds required for it to do it on its own, and an inability to do one thing at a time, so that every journey becomes a phone call opportunity.

Technology is speeding up the world. All over the globe, there has been a massive increase in sales of laptops and mobile phones (with a hands-free set so that you can do something else at the same time); and we wonder however we managed without pagers, remote controls, and e-mail. We live in an instant, insistent world. Advertisements read 'Having trouble keeping up with yourself?' **We yearn for the slower pace of life** we remember in the dim and distant past, but enthusiastically sign up for e-mail, messaging services, evening classes, even time management classes. The result is parents with **a lack of quality time** to spend with their children, and surveys showing that working couples are seeing less and less of each other these days, and that rows over time spent on domestic chores and childcare are becoming a major cause of marital discord. The idea of doing nothing has become terrifying, a sure sign of worthlessness.

Like any commodity that has become scarce, **time has become a battleground**. In what is supposed to be the world of the consumer, firms are stealing time from customers. It is now perfectly acceptable to be asked to hold **the instant** the phone is answered. This saves the company time, but costs you time. We are engaged in a constant, subtle war over time. If politics of class dominated the last century, the politics of time could dominate this one.

Of course, there is a class dimension to the rush culture. One of the biggest transitions of the past few decades has been to take the previous relationship between time and status – the rich had lots of time, the poor had little – and reverse it. While bankers in the City are now at their desk at 7 a.m., in the good old days 'bankers' hours' meant 10 a.m. till 4 p.m. with a decent lunch break. Moreover, to be seen to have time to spare is a sign of low status; when arranging lunch, **it is not done** to be available too soon. Similarly, being late is moving from being a sign of rudeness to a sign of status.

A two-tier time society is gradually being built, with the money-rich, time-poor on one level, and the money-poor, time-rich on the other. The rich are working longer and longer hours in order to compete with each other. At the same time, they are employing others – cleaners, nannies, childminders, gardeners, and fast food outlets – in order to allow them to work all the time. Meanwhile, more and more of us are putting ourselves on **the treadmill of constant activity**, taking on an increasingly heavy workload, and never stopping for a moment to ask ourselves why.

The Observer

3 Read the text again and explain the expressions in **bold**.

4 In pairs, find ...

1 two examples of 'hurry sickness'.
2 five examples of time-saving technology.
3 three consequences of not having enough time.
4 one example of how companies steal time from customers.
5 two situations where having no spare time has become a sign of status.

5 Do you agree with the writer? Why / why not?

Vocabulary
Expressions connected with time

1 Choose the correct word or words. In pairs, check what the expressions mean in a dictionary.

1 Let's go out for a drink **for** (**old** / **past**) **times' sake**.
2 We're living in rented accommodation **for the time** (**present** / **being**).
3 I haven't seen Rob **for** (**donkey's** / **elephant's**) **years**.
4 I don't remember that song – it was **before my** (**time** / **times**), I'm afraid.
5 We arrived at the station just (**in** / **on**) **the nick of time**.
6 The pace of life was slower **in** (**the past** / **former times**).
7 We had to get up **at the** (**crack** / **scratch**) **of dawn** to catch the plane.
8 She decided to go to Paris **on the** (**impulse** / **spur**) **of the moment**.
9 The coach will leave at five o'clock **on the** (**point** / **dot**).
10 It's (**high time** / **more than time**) we bought new carpets.

2 Choose four expressions and make true example sentences.

Multi-word verbs

> We enthusiastically **sign up for** time management classes …
> Having trouble **keeping up with** yourself?

1 ⏱ **Against the clock!** In pairs, you have eight minutes to read the text, find the ten multi-word verbs, and explain their meaning.

I'm a great procrastinator. I always put off doing today what I could do tomorrow. I never seem to get round to writing long and important letters or paying outstanding bills. The problem is, my life is just too hectic; all the work piles up, and I find I can't keep up with all the things I have to do. I quite often fall behind with my paperwork and have to spend the weekend catching up. I'd love to be able to just potter about and linger over reading the papers and having my meals. Perhaps when I retire I'll be able to slow down, but until then I can't see the pressure easing off.

2 In two groups, **A** and **B**, write five questions about someone's lifestyle, using the verbs in **1**.

3 In **A / B** pairs, ask and answer.

Language work
Describing trends

1 **Focus on form** Try to complete the extracts from the text in *Reading* without looking.
- All over the world, people _____ longer and longer hours, and _____ to fit more and more into every day.
- Couples _____ less and less of each other these days.
- A two-tier time society _____ .
- More and more of us are _____ an increasingly heavy workload, and _____ for a moment to ask ourselves why.

1 Which verb form is used in all the sentences? Why?
2 What's the difference between …?
   - A lot of people **commute** to London.
   - A lot of people **are commuting** to London.
3 What comparative forms can be used to talk about an ongoing trend?

2 Choose the alternative in **A** and **B** which is true for your country.

A 1 A great many young people **use / are using** mobile phones.
   2 A large number of women **go / are going** out to work.
   3 Many people **use / are using** credit cards as a means of payment.
   4 Many couples **choose / are choosing** to live together without marrying.
   5 People **eat / are eating** a lot of convenience food.

B 1 Couples are tending to have **more and more / fewer and fewer** children.
   2 Flights are becoming **increasingly / less and less** affordable.
   3 The gap between rich and poor is getting **wider and wider / smaller and smaller**.
   4 The cost of living is getting **higher and higher / lower and lower**.
   5 The pace of life is getting **faster and faster / slower and slower**.

Pronunciation

1 How would you describe your pronunciation of English?
   a It's almost like a native speaker's.
   b It's mainly clear and comprehensible.
   c It's OK but sometimes hard to understand.
2 What sort of pronunciation would you like to have?
3 In pairs, decide on strategies for improving your pronunciation.

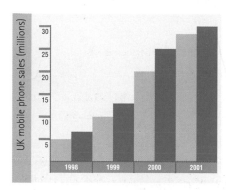

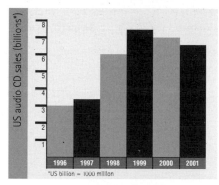

*US billion = 1000 million

English in use
Describing increase and decrease

There has been a	dramatic	increase	in	mobile phone sales.
There was a	sharp	rise		the number of people buying
	steady	decrease		mobile phones.
	slight	drop		

Sales of mobile phones		(have / has)	increased.
The number of people buying			doubled / trebled.
mobile phones			fluctuated.
			remained constant.
			decreased.
			dropped.

1 In pairs, use the expressions in the box to describe the graphs.

2 Talk about changes in consumer behaviour in your country.
   • mobile phones • home computers • food shopping • cars

3 In two groups, **A** and **B**, check the pronunciation and meaning of your words as nouns and verbs in a dictionary. Notice how the main stress is marked.

A		**B**	
rebel	conscript	insult	progress
desert	conduct	protest	extract
decrease	project	convert	refund
produce	contract	reject	convict

4 ⊙2 Listen and check.

5 In **A** / **B** pairs, test each other by giving definitions of words from your list.

Speak out

1 In groups of four, choose one of these topics each and make notes on recent trends in your country.
   • technology • education • leisure • work • family life

2 Take it in turns to present your opinions in one minute. For each presentation, nominate a monitor to note down the expressions used to describe trends. After each presentation, discuss the ideas put forward, and give your own opinion. Find out from the monitor how many different expressions you used.

Remember

• Use a range of language to describe recent and ongoing trends.

• Use phrases to express increase and decrease.

• Use expressions and multi-word verbs connected with time.

Follow-up

1 Write a paragraph about a recent trend in your country.

2 Research idioms connected with time and add them to your vocabulary book.

3 Interview someone about how they use their time, using some of the language in this unit. Note down their replies.

03
FOOD FOR THOUGHT

In this lesson

- Listen to fast colloquial speech.
- Focus on describing habits.
- Talk about food and eating patterns.

Speak for yourself

1 Read this questionnaire. Tick (✓) the option which best describes you.

1 **How important is food to you?**
- Food is one of life's great pleasures.
- I enjoy good food, but it's not a priority for me.
- I eat to live.

2 **How fussy are you about your food?**
- I'll eat anything.
- There are certain foods I prefer to avoid.
- I'm a very picky eater.

3 **How do you feel about cooking?**
- I never cook if I can help it.
- I don't mind cooking but I'm not wild about it either.
- I adore cooking and entertaining.

4 **How often do you eat out?**
- As often as possible.
- From time to time.
- Once in a blue moon.

5 **What is your attitude to food additives?**
- I only eat organically-produced foods.
- I try to avoid foods with flavourings and preservatives.
- It never occurs to me to read food labels.

6 **How important are meal times to you?**
- I like to linger over my meals.
- I tend not to spend a long time over eating.
- I generally grab something quickly on the go.

7 **How often do you nibble between meals?**
- Hardly ever.
- Quite often.
- Constantly.

8 **How health-conscious are you?**
- I tend to eat quite a lot of unhealthy food.
- I try not to eat food that isn't good for me.
- I've no idea what constitutes a healthy diet.

2 In pairs, guess how your partner answered. Discuss your answers.

Did you notice...?

💬 Well, there's, like, my mum, my brother, and me and, like, we almost never eat together.

Like here is an example of a filler. Fillers are words or phrases that are often used in fast speech to give the speaker thinking time.

Listening
Fast, colloquial speech

1 🔘1 Listen to two people talking about issues connected with eating. Note down the problems each person mentions.

2 🔘2 Listen to a sixteen-year-old schoolgirl talking about eating habits in her family.
   - Which of the problems mentioned above does her story illustrate?
   - Do you sympathize with her? Why / why not?

3 🔘3 Listen to the same girl describing an incident involving her brother.
   - What is the main point of the story?
   - Listen again. Which fillers can you hear?

4 Turn to the Tapescript on *p.110*, listen again, and underline the fillers.

5 Listen again without the Tapescript. Can you understand the story better?

6 **What do you think?** In pairs, ask and answer the questions.
   1 Do you think children these days have a less healthy diet than in the past?
   2 In your country, do people generally sit down together and eat as a family? Is this an important part of family life? Why / why not?
   3 Whose responsibility is it to give advice on healthy eating?

Vocabulary
Adjectives to describe food

1 In pairs, decide which adjectives in the box have a negative meaning. Check in a dictionary.

greasy	stodgy	plain	tasty	rich
sickly	tough	overcooked	light	raw
juicy	bland	tender	overripe	fresh

Pronunciation

Look at a copy of the phonemic chart of sounds in English.

1 Do you know which sounds are represented by the symbols?

2 Which words are represented by the symbols below?

1	/fuːd/	7	/ˈtʃɒklət/
2	/iːt/	8	/blænd/
3	/kʊk/	9	/rɪtʃ/
4	/ˈhʌngri/	10	/ˈdʒuːsi/
5	/ˈθɜːsti/	11	/dɪˈzɜːt/
6	/rɔː/	12	/fɪʃ/

2 Find adjectives from 1 which mean ...

heavy and fattening	containing a lot of butter, cream, eggs, etc.
lacking in flavour	not cooked at all
difficult to chew	cooked in too much fat or oil
too sweet	prepared in a simple way / not rich

/ə/ is the most common sound in British English. It never occurs in a stressed syllable.

1 Mark the /ə/ sounds in these words.

butter	seldom
important	entertain
pronunciation	potato
adore	together
margarine	occasionally
interesting	banana

2 [○4] Listen and check.

3 Listen again and repeat.

3 ⏱ **Against the clock!** In pairs, you have three minutes to decide which adjectives from **1** can be used to describe ...

- fruit
- meat
- cakes
- vegetables
- fish
- salad
- bread
- chips
- biscuits
- cheese

4 These adjectives all mean that something is 'past its sell-by date'. Which foods can they describe?

stale	rotten	off	mouldy

5 In pairs, describe a meal you have had in a restaurant or at someone's house. Use a range of adjectives to comment on each course.

Food idioms

1 In pairs, choose the correct explanation for the idioms in **bold**.

1 It's **not my cup of tea**.
 a It's not the kind of thing I like.
 b It's someone else's responsibility.

2 That will give him **food for thought**.
 a That will make him think more clearly.
 b That will give him a lot to think about.

3 You'll find that windsurfing is **a piece of cake**.
 a You'll enjoy it.
 b You'll find it easy.

4 She's **the breadwinner** in the family.
 a She earns the main salary.
 b She works the hardest.

5 **I've got a lot on my plate** at the moment.
 a I'm very busy.
 b I'm enjoying life.

6 That's a **half-baked** idea.
 a It's a ridiculous idea.
 b It's not been thought through very carefully.

7 **Buttering me up** will get you nowhere.
 a You won't get what you want by telling me lies.
 b You won't get what you want by flattery.

8 She's **out to lunch** most of the time.
 a She concentrates hard.
 b She's slightly mad.

9 He's got **a sweet tooth**.
 a He likes sweet food.
 b He always talks nicely to people.

10 He **gets paid peanuts**.
 a His salary is low.
 b He gets a lot of extra benefits.

2 Do the idioms have an equivalent in your language?

English in use
Describing habits

💬 We'll eat watching the telly together.

💬 My husband generally tends to come in quite late.

💬 I go through phases of skipping lunch.

💬 I tend not to eat out during the week.

💬 He never gets to eat anything but snacks.

💬 We almost never eat together.

1 Focus on form In pairs, decide how / when the forms on *p.12* describing habits are used.

2 Use the different forms to talk about your habits relating to ...
- physical exercise
- television
- travel to work / school
- daily routines

Adverbs and adverbial phrases of frequency

never	rarely	sometimes	usually	always

3 ☀ **Against the clock!** In pairs, you have three minutes to position these adverbs and adverbial phrases on the frequency scale above.

once in a blue moon	every now and again	once in a while
as a rule	from time to time	nine times out of ten
every so often	hardly ever	seldom
rarely, if ever	occasionally	generally

4 Where do they go in a sentence?

5 In groups of three, describe what you do / don't do on Sundays.

Speak out

1 In groups of three, describe your eating habits. Talk about ...
- the types of food you eat or don't eat.
- mealtimes: where, what time, how long, and who with.
- eating out and cooking.

2 Ask questions after each person has finished speaking. Take it in turns to monitor, and tick (✓) every time a point from the *Remember* box is used correctly.

3 Think about your own country and others you have visited. Decide which has ...
- the healthiest diet.
- the tastiest food.
- the most sensible mealtimes and eating habits.

Remember
- Use *will / tend to / go through phases of + ing*, and the present simple to describe habits.
- Use a range of adverbs and adverbial phrases of frequency.
- Use different adjectives to describe food.
- Concentrate on the correct pronunciation of words with the /ə/ sound.

Follow-up

1 Imagine you have applied to join a fitness club and you have been asked to describe your lifestyle on an application form. Write about your habits in one paragraph.

2 Visit a local bar or restaurant with another class member. Make notes on the food, service and atmosphere, in preparation for giving a spoken review in class.

3 Study the rules for the position of adverbs in a grammar book. Make notes on anything new you learn.

4 Design a survey to find out about food and eating in different parts of the world.

04
SO WHAT IS IT YOU DO?

In this lesson

- Talk about jobs, studies, plans, and ambitions.
- Practise using verb / noun collocations.
- Focus on verb forms to talk about jobs and current projects.

Did you notice...?

Why did Russell say ...

👄 *I work within the mediums of film and photography.*

but talk about ...?

👄 *a film that I'm working on ...*

Speak for yourself

What questions would you ask the people in the photos about their jobs / studies?

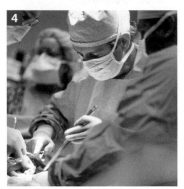

Listening
Focusing on verb forms

1 💿1 Listen to Mark asking Russell about his job. Note down the questions he asks.

2 Listen again. Note down what Russell says about ...
- his work in general. • his current project.

3 💿2 Listen to Mark talking about his work.
1 What two jobs does he do?
2 How does he describe doing two jobs at once? Why?

4 **Focus on form** Read the transcript of Mark describing his job. Which forms of the verbs in brackets complete the text?

....

I work with all kinds of household name businesses over here and I usually work with small groups of managers in the area of improving communication, er, communications, inter-relations, er, team-building, problem-solving, that type of area, um, and I [1] _____ (do) that for about twenty years or so. But I [2] _____ (always / be) musical, and I [3] _____ (be) a performer in the past, and about seven or eight years ago I [4] _____ (start) composing ... and, um, I [5] _____ (do) bits for the BBC, I [6] _____ (do) a wildlife series a few months ago.

....

5 Listen again and check. Why are these verb forms used?

💬 *So what do you do?*

💬 *So how long have you been doing that?*

What is the reason for using *So* at the beginning of a question?

English in use
Asking about jobs and studies

💬 *So what is it that you do?*

1 ☀ **Against the clock!** You have two minutes to predict the questions.
   1 What _____ a living, then?
   2 What have _____ work-wise?
   3 So how long _____ ?
   4 How's _____ going?
   5 How did _____ , then?

2 🔲 Listen and check.

3 Listen again. Note down three useful expressions from the responses.

4 🔲 Listen to someone asking a teenager about their studies. Did you ask the same questions in *Speak for yourself*?

5 In pairs, ask and answer about your own jobs or studies.

Pronunciation

1 🔲 Listen and write down the words you hear.

2 Which sound do they have in common? How many different ways is it spelt?

3 Listen again and practise repeating the words.

4 Think of five other words with the same sound.

Vocabulary
Collocations

1 Complete with the correct form of a single or multi-word verb.
   1 I'm planning to _____ freelance in March.
   2 Hopefully I'll _____ promoted when my boss retires.
   3 When I've _____ my degree, I'd like to _____ advertising.
   4 My ambition is to _____ my own business.
   5 I'm fed up with the commuting, so I'm planning to _____ my notice.
   6 I'm hoping I won't _____ redundant when the firm is downsized.
   7 I'm going to _____ six months' maternity leave after the baby's born.
   8 I'm toying with the idea of _____ early retirement next year.

2 In pairs, ask and answer about your plans and ambitions using verb / noun collocations.

Speak out

1 In pairs, **A** look at *p.103* and **B** look at *p.107*. Check the meaning of any new words in a dictionary.
   1 Ask **B** about his / her job. Say what you think it involves.
   2 **B** confirm or correct **A**'s ideas. Swap roles.

   A *So what do you do for a living?*
   B *I'm a sound engineer for MGM films.*
   A *Oh, right. So does that mean you actually record the actors?*
   B *Well, not exactly. My job involves working in a studio and editing.*

2 Make similar conversations with ideas of your own.

Remember
- Ask questions and show interest to keep the conversation going.
- Use a range of expressions to ask about jobs and ambitions.
- Use correct verb forms to talk about jobs and current projects.
- Use verb / noun collocations to talk about jobs and studies.

05
LOVE AT FIRST SIGHT?

In this lesson

- Read to pick out key points.
- Look at expressions and multi-word verbs connected with relationships.
- Practise paying compliments.
- Focus on *so*, *such*, and *really*.

Pronunciation

1 Mark the stress on the words in these word families.

advert	photo
advertise	photograph
advertising	photography
advertisement	photographer
psychology	biology
psychologist	biologist
psychological	biological
organize	person
organizer	personal
organization	personality

2 🔊1 Listen and check. What do you notice about the position of the stressed syllable?

3 Listen again and practise repeating the word groups.

Speak for yourself

1 Do you believe in love at first sight? Has it ever happened to you or people you know?

2 In pairs, decide what initially attracts one person to another.

3 Read the extract. Do you agree with the psychologists?

> It seems that love at first sight – eyes meeting across a crowded room – is not just the stuff of romantic novels; it is a scientifically-recognized phenomenon. According to research carried out by psychologists, when we meet someone, it takes us only a few seconds to make up our minds if we are attracted to them and to weigh up their suitability as a prospective mate. Appearance and body language are what we look at first of all, but we can also pick up important clues as to a person's background and personality from their voice and the way they speak.

4 In two groups, **A** and **B**, match your words below.

A		B	
blind	hearts	eligible	office
lonely	bar	arranged	Right
lifelong	date	Mr	ceremony
soul	commitment	registry	bachelor
singles	mate	civil	marriage

5 **A** turn to *p.103*, and **B** to *p.107*. Check your expressions and in **A / B** pairs, ask and answer the questions.

Reading
Taking notes

1 In three groups, **A**, **B**, and **C**, **A** read **Text A** opposite, **B** turn to *p.103*, and **C** to *p.107*. Make notes to answer your questions.

2 In groups of three, tell someone from another group about your text, using the notes you have made as prompts.

3 **What do you think?** Which of the ways of meeting a partner is most and least likely to lead to a lasting relationship? Why?

HERE'S THE DEAL: WILL YOU MARRY ME?

Lesley Friedman, millionaire and chief executive officer of a New York law firm, describes her quest to find a soul mate. 'I was over forty and unattached, and I thought, "I have been a very successful entrepreneur. What if I approached dating the way I approached my business?"' So she mapped out her five-year plan: find the right market for your product; re-image the product if current image is not working; network; ask for the order; close the deal and get married.

The easiest part was step one, the market component. Friedman is looking for an intelligent, highly motivated man aged forty plus, so she zeroed in on high-brow charities and political fund-raisers. Step two, re-imaging, was where she ran into problems. The transformation itself was a wild success. On the advice of friends and a trainer, she lost two stone, hired a consultant to revamp her wardrobe from dowdy to sexy, straightened and cut her hair, and replaced her glasses with contact lenses. 'I wanted to be judged on my achievements', she says. 'But I found that while women look for their mental and emotional peer in a partner, men focus on looks and chemistry first. So I finally decided that yes, changing my looks was superficial and against my feminist instincts, but I am forty-something and want to get married.'

Friedman also began networking (step three) by attending balls and fund-raising events, but found that step four (ask for the order) was the key to success. It's the reason she has had 150 dates in the past two years, spawning six relationships and one proposal of marriage (which she turned down). 'In business, you can't have a pleasant talk with the buyer and leave it at that. To close the deal, you have to ask for the order. You have to ask your friends to fix you up, to make the sale. You have to be introduced to men. And if one date doesn't work out, you go out and get another.'

Now near the end of year two in her five-year plan, Friedman is still single, enthusiastic, and hopeful. Women applaud her, while men are either intrigued or intimidated. 'There are some people who find what I am doing wrong. They say to me, "Lesley, you should wait to be chosen", but I don't think so. See you at the wedding!'

---

two stone = 12.7 kg

1 How successful was each of the five steps in Friedman's plan, and why?
2 How have other people reacted to her plan?

Did you notice...?

💬 *But I decided I wanted to meet a partner like this because ...*

💬 *I was over 40 and unattached.*

There are various ways of talking about people's relationship status. What do these expressions mean?

- my other half
- a single parent
- we're going out together
- we're living together
- my ex
- a spouse

Vocabulary
Expressions and multi-word verbs

1 In two groups, **A** and **B**, look at the expressions in your column. Try to explain their meaning. Check in a dictionary.

A	B
have an affair with	hit it off with
think the world of	be infatuated with
be on the same wavelength as	be crazy about
have a crush on	have a fling with
have a soft spot for	be seeing someone
not see eye to eye with	be unfaithful to
flirt with	play hard to get

2 In **A** / **B** pairs, test your partner on the expressions in your column.

3 ☀ **Against the clock!** You have four minutes to complete the sentences with the correct words.

1 I didn't use to like Emma but she's beginning to grow _____ me.
2 Matt and Jo have split _____ . I thought they were getting on well.
3 I didn't take _____ her at first but now we're really close.
4 Who was that girl you were chatting _____ in the bar last night?
5 Tom fell _____ _____ Alex and now they're not speaking.
6 They had a terrible row last week but I think they've made _____ now.
7 I'm not sure Jenny will ever get _____ Philip. He meant the world to her.
8 I used to really fancy James but I've gone _____ him recently.

4 Use some of the expressions and multi-word verbs you didn't know before to describe relationships you or your friends have had.

Pronunciation

1 Mark the words with the main stress in the compliments below.
2 ○2 Listen and check.
3 Listen again and repeat.

English in use
Paying compliments

1 Which responses are possible for each compliment?

2 Would you make the same responses? Why / why not?

Language work

So, such, and really

1 Focus on form Complete these rules.

Use *so* before
Use *such (a)* before
Use *really* before

- adjective
- adverb

- adjective + noun
- 'positive' or 'negative' noun

2 Look at the cartoons and decide what the people are saying.

Speak out

1 a Prepare compliments to pay to others in the class. Think about ...
- clothes · appearance · skills · talents
- recent achievements · personal qualities

b ● **Against the clock!** You have five minutes to go round the class and pay compliments. Respond in an appropriate way.

2 a Look at the statements. Choose one you agree with and one you disagree with, and prepare your ideas.

> **You should wait till you are in your thirties before getting married.**
>
> ## Marriage was easier in my parents' days.
>
> Shared interests are the most important element in a relationship.
>
> # True love lasts forever.
>
> Divorce is better than an unhappy marriage.
>
> ## Getting married is better than living together.

b In groups of four, talk about the statements you chose and why you agree / disagree with them.

Remember
- For **1a** and **b**, use a range of expressions with *so*, *such*, and *really* to pay compliments.
- For **2a** and **b**, use a wide range of expressions and multi-word verbs to talk about relationships.

Follow-up

1 Look in an English-language newspaper / magazine and find the Lonely Hearts column. Find out the meanings of any abbreviations used, and look up any words you don't know. Choose the most suitable partner for you!

2 Write the ad that you would place in a Lonely Hearts column.

3 Make a word diagram to link words and expressions connected with love and romance in your vocabulary book.

4 Look up derivatives of six of the words in this unit. Note these in your vocabulary book, and mark the stress on each one.

06
HERE IS THE NEWS

In this lesson

- Listen to understand news bulletins.
- Study the use of articles.
- Focus on two-part nouns.
- Practise giving and reacting to news.

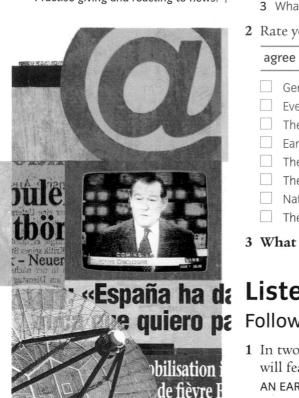

Speak for yourself

1 In pairs, ask and answer.

1 How often do you read or listen to the news?

2 Do you prefer to follow the news on TV, on the radio, or in newspapers? Why?

3 What proportion of news in your country is devoted to international affairs?

2 Rate your opinion for each statement.

agree	1	2	3	4	5	disagree

- ☐ Genetically modified foods should be banned.
- ☐ Everyone should have the right to freedom of expression.
- ☐ The benefits of nuclear power outweigh the risks.
- ☐ Earthquakes often cause more death and destruction than is necessary.
- ☐ There is no point in going on a demonstration.
- ☐ The developed countries should cancel debts owed by poorer countries.
- ☐ National industries should not be sold off to foreign companies.
- ☐ The private lives of politicians do not concern the public.

3 What do you think? Choose three of the topics to discuss in pairs.

Listening
Following news bulletins

1 In two groups, **A** and **B**, predict which words / phrases from your box will feature in which news story.

AN EARTHQUAKE   A DEMONSTRATION   THE INTERNET   THE CAR INDUSTRY

A					
unions	management	casualties	rally	abolition	rubble
clashed	death toll	censor	crackdown	detained	providers

A POLITICAL SCANDAL   GM FOODS   DEVELOPING COUNTRIES   NUCLEAR POWER

B					
ingredients	stand down	leak	resignation	eliminate	donated
allegations	eradication	brand	crops	aid	plant

2 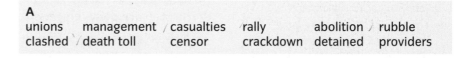 Listen to your bulletins and note down the main point of each story.

3 Within your group, compare your ideas. Listen again and check.

4 In **A / B** pairs, tell your partner about two or three of the stories that you heard.

Apparently, ...
I heard on the news that ...

5 🔊 Listen to five more stories and note down key words / phrases.

6 In pairs, summarize the five stories in one sentence each.

7 Which verb forms in *Did you notice ...?* are used ...
- to announce recent news?
- to add further details, especially regarding time and place?
- to make announcements about the near future in informal speech?
- to make announcements about the near future in formal speech?

Did you notice...?

💬 The Foreign Secretary has resigned.

💬 He handed in his resignation earlier today.

💬 I've just been given the sack.

💬 BLC is to eliminate GM ingredients.

💬 The Bank of England will make an announcement later today.

💬 Jenny's going to have a baby.

You can use a range of verb forms to make announcements.

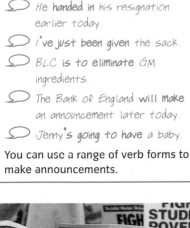

Vocabulary
Two-part nouns

💬 The government has announced a **crackdown** on the publication of offensive literature.

💬 There was a reported **breakdown** in a nuclear power station.

1 Read the sentences. Match the nouns in **bold** with the definitions.
1 And we'll be bringing you an **update** on that story later on.
2 Relief workers are struggling to prevent an **outbreak** of cholera.
3 The Prime Minister has suffered a **setback** in his electoral campaign.
4 There has been a **breakthrough** in talks on the future of the car industry.
5 The low **turnout** at the conference may have been due to the weather.
6 Car workers have been asked to double **output** by the end of the year.
7 The government is to announce **cutbacks** in its education budget.
8 The **outcome** of the talks will be known later today.
9 The company has an annual **turnover** of £400 million.
10 There are fears of a **backlash** against the government by the rebel forces.

a number of people attending
b amount of production
c result of something
d amount of business
e problem that delays progress
f sudden start of something
g important new development
h reduction in something
i negative reaction to something
j account of recent developments

2 Which part of the nouns is stressed? Practise saying them.

3 In pairs, choose four of the nouns and write example sentences.

4 In groups of four, read out your examples without the noun for the other pair to complete.

Language work
Uses of the definite and indefinite article

1 ☀ **Against the clock!** You have two minutes to complete the text with *a*, *an*, *the*, or no article.

> [1] _____ pet cat has survived after going through [2] _____ complete washing cycle in [3] _____ automatic washing machine. [4] _____ cat's owner had said he didn't realize that [5] _____ cat was in [6] _____ machine when he loaded it up before going to [7] _____ work. [8] _____ cat is reported to be dazed but unharmed.

2 [○3] Listen and check your answers. In pairs, decide on rules to explain your decisions.

3 Tick the letter(s) to complete this rule correctly.
We almost always use a determiner (*a* / *the* / *my* / *this* / *that*) before …
a singular countable nouns
b plural nouns
c uncountable nouns

Forming noun phrases

> Look at these examples
>
> | A | B |
> | --- | --- |
> | offensive literature is published | **the** publication **of** offensive literature |
> | student grants will be abolished | **the** abolition **of** student grants |

4 Look at the headlines below and describe the topic of the stories. Use a noun phrase instead of a verb.
Cézanne masterpiece stolen.
The story is about the theft of a Cézanne masterpiece.

Pronunciation

1 Read the story in **1** again. In pairs, decide which words are stressed and where the pauses are.

2 Listen again and check.

3 Practise reading with the tape.

4 Practise reading to each other. Monitor stress and pauses.

Hospital wards to be closed

1,000 HECTARES LOST IN FIRE

Scientists discover AIDS vaccine

GM foods to be eradicated

2,000 new homes to be built

GOVERNMENT TO LAUNCH NEW DRUGS INITIATIVE

Car plant will create about 1,000 jobs

Pop star mysteriously disappears

What a nightmare!

Congratulations!

English in use
Giving and reacting to news

1 ⊙4 Listen to seven conversation openings. In each case, predict what the listener will say next.

2 ⊙5 Listen and check your predictions.

3 Turn to the Tapescript on *p.112* and find expressions used to ...

a introduce news   d respond to bad news

b respond to good news   e express lack of surprise

c express surprise   f show interest

4 ⦿ **Against the clock!** You have three minutes to match these expressions to the categories in **3**.

How annoying!	I'm so sorry.
That's hardly surprising.	Congratulations!
According to the *Independent*, ...	Oh, right.
That's incredible!	He didn't!
Well done!	Really?
What a nightmare!	That makes a change!
What a pity!	Apparently, ...
They haven't, have they?	Wow! That's fantastic!
You must be thrilled.	Good for him!

Speak out

1 Prepare to exchange personal, local, national, or international news. Look at the categories below and make notes on some of them.

  1 News about yourself, family members, friends, and acquaintances.
- jobs
- relationships
- celebrations
- pets
- holidays
- houses
- purchases
- hobbies

  2 News about your school, university, or workplace.
- staff changes
- courses
- working practices
- buildings
- exams
- social events

  3 News you've heard on the TV or radio, or read in the newspapers.
- political news
- local news
- international events
- celebrities
- entertainment
- sport

2 Move around the class exchanging news. Ask questions and repeat news you have heard from other class members.

3 In groups of four, share the most interesting pieces of news.

Pronunciation

1 ⊙6 Listen to the stress and intonation of some of the expressions in *English in use* 4. Mark the stressed words.

2 Listen again and repeat.

Remember

- Use a range of expressions for giving and reacting to news.
- Concentrate on the correct use of articles.
- Use some two-part nouns.

Follow-up

1 Study a news item (from the radio, TV, or newspaper) and prepare to summarize it in the next lesson.

2 Look at the Tapescript of the news bulletins on *pp.111/112* and note down useful words / multi-word expressions in your vocabulary book.

3 Write a local news item for a bulletin and practise saying it. In class, record a news programme including some of the bulletins.

4 Prepare three pieces of personal, local, national, or international news to bring to the next lesson.

Speak for yourself

☀ **Against the clock!** In pairs, you have five minutes to improvise four of these conversations.

1 Ask a stranger for directions to the station.
2 Ask a friend for someone's phone number.
3 Ask a stranger questions about the bus service.
4 Ask for details of accommodation at a tourist information bureau.
5 Phone a cinema to ask about performance times.
6 Phone the electricity board to make an inquiry about your electricity bill.
7 Ask a colleague for a phone number.

Listening
Noting the exact words

1 ⊙1 Listen to eight short conversations in which people are asking for information. Say …
- where each conversation is taking place.
- what information is asked for.

2 Listen again. Complete these requests for information.

1 Hi Paul, _____ ?   5 _____ Hayfield Road.
    _____ she'll be back?   6 _____ to Manchester.

2 _____ , do you?   7 _____ about car hire.
    _____ Personnel?   _____ it opens?

3 _____ the London train?   8 _____ about rubbish

4 _____ round here?   collection.
    _____ vegan food too?

3 **What do you think?** Would you make requests in a similar way in your language? Did you make similar requests in *Speak for yourself*?

English in use
Asking for information

Start conversations politely

Excuse me, ...
Sorry to trouble you, ...
I wonder if you could help me.

State your purpose

I'm looking for (information about) ...
I'm ringing to enquire about ...
I'd like to speak to someone about ...

Use indirect questions

Could you tell me ...
Do you happen to know ...

Against the clock! In pairs, you have four minutes to decide how these questions might continue.

1 (At work) Any idea what time ...?
2 (On a train) Do you happen to know if ...?
3 (At a restaurant) Could you tell me where ...?
4 (At a bus stop) I don't suppose you'd happen to know when ...?
5 (In a shop) Any idea whether ...?
6 (At a railway station) Could you tell me how long ...?

Did you notice...?

· Use *may*, *might*, or *could* to indicate uncertainty about the past, present, or future.

   💬 Tim **might** know.

   💬 She **may** have popped out.

· Use *should* or *ought to* to express a tentative conclusion.

   💬 Personnel **ought to** know.

   💬 She **should** be back by then.

Answer the questions in the *Vocabulary* section using *may*, *might*, *could*, *should*, or *ought to*.

Vocabulary
Colloquial responses

Complete the responses. How certain is the speaker in each response?

1 'Do you know if they take credit cards?' 'Sorry, I _____ a clue.'
2 'Do you know how often the buses run?' 'Sorry, _____ offhand.'
3 'How long is the interval?' 'About twenty minutes, as far as I _____ .'
4 'Do you know where the leisure centre is?' 'Sorry, I've no _____ .'
5 'Do you know Adrian's date of birth?' 'Not off the _____ of my head.'
6 'Have you any idea where the Majestic Restaurant is?' 'No, never _____ of it, sorry.'
7 'Do you know if the post has gone?' 'Sorry, I haven't the _____ idea.'
8 'What flavour is this ice cream?' 'I've _____ idea.'
9 'Is the trip fully booked?' 'I'm pretty _____ there are spaces left.'
10 'Where's Carol?' 'I've a _____ she's gone to the dentist's.'

Remember

· Use a range of expressions to ask for information.
· Use colloquial responses where possible.
· Concentrate on word linking.

Speak out

1 In pairs, repeat the conversations you had in *Speak for yourself* and improvise the others.

2 Write down five pieces of information to get from others in the class. Move around the class, asking and answering questions.

Speak for yourself

If you could go anywhere in the world for a holiday, where would you go?

Reading

Following a guidebook entry

1 Have you ever been to India? If so, what were your impressions? If not, what sights and sensations would you expect to find?

2 ⏱ **Against the clock!** You have three minutes to match the adjectives in **A** with the nouns in **B**.

A	B		A	B
vibrant	reality		contrasting	peaks
barren	palm groves		lush	landscapes
tranquil	colours		snow-capped	filth
unspoilt	aroma		shocking	paddy fields
harsh	beaches		rolling	spices
fragrant	deserts		exotic	hills

3 Read the text and check your answers. Which of your ideas from **1** were mentioned?

4 **What do you think?** Read the article again.
   1 Underline any features of life in India that particularly appeal to you.
   2 In pairs, compare your ideas.

India
LAND OF CONTRASTS

There's nowhere quite like India: the heady concoction of all that is beautiful in the world, and the harsh reality of a country that is home to around 900 million people.

To paint India as only a romantic destination would be painfully superficial. There are such extremes of poverty and wealth in this vast, vast subcontinent that it would be callous just to talk of the incredible sunrises and sunsets over the Taj Mahal. A holiday in India would undoubtedly take in fabulously romantic sights, but no visit to India can gloss over the shocking filth, poverty, continual hassle and throngs of people that is part of life. Despite all this, perhaps because of all the hassles, people fall deeply in love with this fascinating country, and long to return again and again.

The subcontinent has a life of its own – from the haggling buyers and sellers to the passionately revered cows in the streets, along with the vibrant colours and fragrant aroma of the flower garlands and the mounds of exotic spices piled up in the markets. It is also steeped in a complex history stretching back over 4,000 years, during which the philosophies, religions, and languages of its people have expanded to produce the immense wealth of culture, heritage, and tradition that exists there today.

There is no doubt that India's landscapes are overwhelmingly beautiful in their variety. They range from the harsh barren deserts of Rajasthan to the rolling green hills of Darjeeling; from the snow-capped peaks of the Himalayas to the tranquil palm groves and lush paddy fields of the south, to say nothing of the long unspoilt beaches beside the Indian Ocean. You can stay in former palaces, explore hilltop forts, haggle for an auto-rickshaw in Delhi, escape the heat among the tea plantations of Darjeeling, or for those who prefer a more leisurely holiday, you can just relax for a few days on a palm-fringed beach somewhere off the beaten track.

And then there is religion. Apart from the continually contrasting landscapes and the colourful pageant of its people, at the very heart of India is a religious spirit which, more than anything else, is responsible for making the country so magical, so captivating. Indeed, the very essence of India is religion, and the strength of Hinduism and Buddhism, both of which originated there.

The Good Honeymoon Guide

Did you notice...?

💬 This **vast, vast** subcontinent.

💬 People long to return **again** and **again**.

What is the effect of repeating the words in bold?

Vocabulary

Location expressions

💬 *Just relax for a few days on a palm-fringed beach somewhere off the beaten track.*

1 Read these sentences and tick (✓) those which are true for you.
   1 There is a cinema **within walking distance of** my home.
   2 I love spending my holidays **off the beaten track**.
   3 My English school is located **right in the heart of the town**.
   4 I'd hate to live **in the middle of nowhere**.
   5 I live **a couple of minutes' walk from** a bus stop.
   6 It's dangerous to walk alone **in the back streets** of my town.
   7 It's **a ten-minute drive** to the supermarket from where I live.
   8 There's a bank **a few blocks from** here.
   9 I'd like to stay in a hotel that's just **a stone's throw from** the sea.
   10 The nearest airport is only about ten kilometres away **as the crow flies**.

2 In pairs, compare your ideas.

3 ⏱ **Against the clock!** In pairs, you have two minutes to explain the difference between the expressions in bold.
   1 The youth hostel is situated **north of / in the north of** the city.
   2 We stayed in a campsite **on the main road / off the main road**.
   3 We have to go **inland / to the mainland** to do our shopping.
   4 We spent our holiday **on the coast / on the beach**.

4 Use some of the expressions in **1** and **3** to talk about your home, your school, and holidays you have had.

Language work
Expressing preferences

For those who prefer a more leisurely holiday, you can just relax ...

1 Focus on form Complete the sentences with one word.

General preferences

On the whole, I prefer sightseeing _____ sunbathing.
Personally, I like secluded coves _____ than crowded beaches.
I like them both _____ .
I don't like _____ of them.

Making a choice

I think I'd rather go out _____ stay in tonight.
Given the choice, I _____ sooner stay in a hostel than go camping.
On balance, I'd prefer to travel alone _____ than go on a coach tour.
I'd just as _____ go for a week as go for a fortnight.
I don't mind. It's _____ to you.
I'm easy. I'll go _____ you like.

Asking about preferences

Which do you _____ , the seaside or the countryside?
Do you _____ the seaside or the countryside?
What would you _____ do, go for a walk or have a swim?
Would you _____ have a beer or a Coke?

2 In pairs, ask and answer questions about the following topics. Give reasons for your preferences.

General preferences	Making a choice
rugged landscapes / picturesque landscapes	go to an art gallery / visit a monument
beach holidays / city breaks	travel independently / go on a package tour
lively resorts / quiet places	go on holiday alone / go with friends
travelling by train / travelling by car	camp / stay in a hotel

Pronunciation

1 Try saying the *Asking about preferences* questions with the correct intonation.
2 [○1] Listen, check, and repeat.
3 In pairs, practise asking and answering.

English in use
Reaching a decision

1 Read this description of a hotel in India. Would you like to stay there? Why / why not?

WINDAMERE HOTEL

THE most refined and popular place to stay in Darjeeling, the Windamere is the perfect spot if you are looking for a little old world style and relaxation. This wonderful old colonial mansion, set on the slope of Observatory Hill, is just like stepping back in time to the days of the Empire. You'll find no frivolous modern amenities here such as televisions, central heating, or minibars, and the owner of the hotel, Mrs Tenduf-La, a formidable Tibetan octogenarian, is proud of it. Instead, the Windamere has other delights in store for guests, such as open fires lit each night in the guest rooms, hot water bottles, afternoon tea served on the lawn, a string quartet playing in the drawing-room, and a pianist who plays during dinner. The food at the Windamere is excellent, and the portions generous. Bedrooms are basically furnished, with private shower (cold water only) and WC.

Pronunciation

1 🔲3 Listen to extracts from the conversation in **2**. Notice how the speaker's voice changes pitch when he quotes from the text.

2 In pairs, practise quoting from the text about India on *pp.26* and *27*.

💬 It says here, ...
Listen to this ...

2 🔲2 Listen to two people discussing the hotel. Are they enthusiastic?

3 Turn to the Tapescript on *p.112* and listen again. Underline the language they use to express ...
- enthusiasm about something
- lack of enthusiasm about something
- doubt or uncertainty
- a suggestion

4 In pairs, use the expressions to discuss your reactions to the text.

Speak out

1 a In three groups, **A**, **B**, and **C**, **A** look at the hotel information on *p.104*, **B** on *p.107*, and **C** on *p.108*.

b Highlight the points which appeal to you, things that don't appeal, and anything you are uncertain about.

c Compare your ideas with other people in your group.

d In **A** / **B** / **C** groups, tell each other about your hotels, and reach a decision about where to go.

2 In new groups of three or four, imagine you have to make a three-minute promotional video clip for a holiday destination you know. Reach a decision about ...
- what exactly you would show on the clip.
- a running sequence for the video.
- a title.

Remember
- Use different expressions to express enthusiasm, lack of enthusiasm, uncertainty, and to make suggestions.
- Ask and answer about preferences.
- Use a range of location expressions.
- Concentrate on correct intonation to quote from a text and ask about preferences.

Follow-up

1 Produce a poster to advertise your country or another holiday destination, and display it on the classroom wall.

2 Write a voice-over for the promotional video you planned in *Speak out*.

3 Find a description of a famous holiday destination in your country. Prepare to give a short summary to the class, and give your opinion on how accurately it portrays the place.

4 Find a holiday brochure and note the kind of adjective / noun collocations that are commonly used. Start a page in your vocabulary book for adjective / noun collocations.

09
CAUSE FOR CONCERN

In this lesson

- Listen to understand the main points.
- Study and practise expressions connected with crime and quantity.
- Focus on ways of talking about cause, blame, and solutions.
- Practise speaking to solve problems.

Speak for yourself

Westcombe's aim is for young men to leave ...

- more able to take their place in society as husbands, fathers, sons, employees, and citizens.
- more likely to gain employment, enjoy constructive leisure pursuits, and participate in education.
- less likely to reoffend.

DANIEL, AGED 18, serving two years for armed robbery

SOLLY, AGED 19, serving three months for assaulting a rival fan at a football match

CHRIS, AGED 20, serving three years for supplying heroin

What do you think? In pairs, ask and answer these questions.

1 What could have caused the young men to commit these offences?
2 Why do you think the vast majority of young offenders are men?
3 What would happen to them in your country?

Did you notice...?

> Figures have shown ...

> Approximately a third of ...

We use this language to talk about science, medical developments, law and order, developments in your own field, etc.

> It's been proved that ...

> Research has indicated that ...

> According to a recent report ...

Listening
The main points

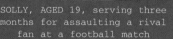 Listen to a probation officer at a prison for young offenders talking about the causes of juvenile crime.

1 Note down the main points he makes. Compare notes with a partner.
2 Turn to the Tapescript on *p.112*. Highlight any multi-word expressions that are new to you.

Vocabulary
Expressions connected with crime

1 Read the text quickly and decide what the main topic is.

2 ☀ **Against the clock!** You have five minutes to complete the text using the expressions from the box.

effective discipline	crime rate	corporal punishment
young offenders	stricter measures	socially deprived
in custody	punishments	patrol the streets
take out their aggression	family breakdown	too lenient
on probation	vandalized	juvenile delinquency

The sight of ¹ _____ telephone booths and bus shelters, slashed tube seats, and walls sprayed with graffiti has become depressingly common. For many people, the rising ² _____ has become a cause of considerable concern. There are those who consider the recent increase in ³ _____ to be due to a lack of ⁴ _____ at home and at school. They maintain that the courts have become far ⁵ _____ with criminals, and that ⁶ _____ should be taken. Police should ⁷ _____ in greater numbers to keep an eye on trouble-makers; and as for youngsters convicted of an offence, putting them ⁸ _____ is no longer enough. It is time, they say, for a return to old-fashioned measures like ⁹ _____ .

Others, however, blame social conditions such as unemployment, poor housing, and ¹⁰ _____ . They say that many ¹¹ _____ , lacking any proper facilities or means of expression, need to let off steam, and so they ¹² _____ on their environment. These people, they say, are ¹³ _____ , and we should be offering them our help and understanding rather than keeping them ¹⁴ _____ and handing out increasingly severe ¹⁵ _____ .

3 In pairs, **A** and **B**, **A** read out the first sentence and pause at the gap. **B** try to remember the expression. Swap roles half-way through.

Language work
Quantity expressions

These expressions are used in more formal English instead of words like *most, many, some,* etc.

a great deal of	the majority of	a large number of
a great many	vast amounts of	a tiny minority of
a certain amount of	a small number of	a small amount of
the vast majority of	the overwhelming majority of	a number of
virtually all	virtually no	

1 ☀ **Against the clock!** You have three minutes to divide the expressions into two groups, according to whether they are used with countable or uncountable nouns. Some can be used with both.

2 Arrange them in order in their groups, from largest to smallest.

3 Which expressions are followed by a plural verb and which by a singular verb?

1 [○2] Listen to eight quantity expressions. Notice the pronunciation of *a*, *the*, and *of*.

2 Listen again and repeat.

3 Talk about class members using some of the quantity expressions on *p.31*. Pay attention to the pronunciation of *a*, *the*, and *of*.

a — What negative things have you learned in prison? ___

b — What kind of work will you do when you leave? ___

c — What positive things can prison offer you? ___

d — So, why are you in here? ___

e — Why is it so important to have a lot of money? ___

4 Complete the sentences with a suitable expression.

1 _____ violent crimes are committed by men.
2 _____ countries impose the death penalty.
3 _____ crimes are related to drugs.
4 _____ juvenile delinquency is caused by family breakdown.
5 _____ judges are women.
6 At present, there is _____ unemployment in my country.
7 _____ crimes remain unresolved each year.
8 _____ people are the victims of burglary each year.
9 There is _____ poverty in my country.
10 _____ violence is shown on TV nowadays.

'Ungrammatical' language

5 [○3] Listen to five extracts from interviews with young offenders. Match the questions to the extracts.

6 What were the answers to the questions? Did they surprise you?

7 **Focus on form** What is 'ungrammatical' about these sentences?

1 I'm in here because I done an armed robbery.
2 I thought I knew it all, but when I come in here, I don't know nothing.
3 We're going to have to do them stupid jobs.
4 You've got work that don't pay you nothing.

English in use
Cause, blame, and solutions

1 Complete the sentences with a suitable word.

Talking about the cause of a problem

I think one reason _____ young people turn to crime is _____ they don't have a job.

The main reason _____ juvenile delinquency is unemployment.

I think the increase in violence is largely / partly / entirely _____ to a lack of recreational facilities.

A key factor _____ juvenile crime is poor parenting.

Talking about blame

I think society as a whole is _____ blame.

I blame the problem _____ television.

I think parents have a lot to answer _____ .

Putting forward solutions

I think / don't think we _____ hand out stricter punishments.

The best solution / One way forward would be _____ schools _____ exercise more discipline.

I think there's a lot / something to be said _____ community service.

1 Try saying these words with the correct stress.

solution	television
expression	institution
conversation	decision
qualification	relation
option	invasion
intonation	education

2 [○4] Listen and check.

3 Listen again and repeat.

4 Think of six other words ending in *-tion* or *-sion*.

2 In pairs, look at the newspaper headlines and choose three that interest you.

- Decide what the causes of the problem are, and who or what is to blame.
- Suggest solutions.

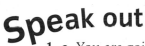

New report shows some dolphins on the verge of extinction

New figures show 50% of marriages end in divorce

PUPILS 'OUT OF CONTROL' SAY SECONDARY SCHOOL TEACHERS

Smoking on the increase in developing countries

POLL REVEALS THAT MOST PEOPLE DON'T KNOW THEIR NEIGHBOURS

Many pupils leave school 'virtually illiterate' say employers

Speak out

1 a You are going to take part in a public meeting to discuss how to tackle the problem of growing levels of juvenile crime. Read the background information below.

BARCHESTER is a medium-sized town which has recently seen a massive increase in violence, and in vandalism, petty theft, burglary, and armed robbery involving young offenders (up to the age of 21). There is a high unemployment rate, and many young people leave school without qualifications. A large number of the offenders come from troubled family backgrounds, and drug abuse is a growing problem. A meeting has been called to decide how to spend a sum of money allocated by the government to deal with the town's crime problems.

b Turn to *p.104* and read the proposed solutions.

c Agree on a time limit as a class. In groups of three, follow this agenda.

1 Discuss the reasons for the recent increase in crime and violence in general.
2 Review the advantages and disadvantages of the proposed solutions.
3 Reach agreement on how the solutions can be implemented.
4 Choose the two best solutions.

2 [○5] Listen to the probation officer giving his opinion on the best way to rehabilitate young offenders.

1 What three solutions does he mention?
2 Do you agree that prison is not the best option?

Remember

- Use a range of expressions to talk about crime, cause, blame, and solutions.
- Use a range of expressions to describe quantity.
- Back up your argument.

Follow-up

1 Find a newspaper report of a crime, and underline any new multi-word expressions.
2 Write a short letter to a newspaper, saying who you think is to blame for a problem that is in the news, and explaining your idea for a solution.
3 Prepare to give a short speech on a topic that gives you cause for concern.

10
WHERE WAS I?

In this lesson

- Talk about cross-cultural differences.
- Practise interrupting and returning to a topic.
- Look at vocabulary connected with body language.

Speak for yourself

1 Read the questionnaire. Tick (✓) the option which best describes you.

1 When you want to say something in class, do you ...
- speak out immediately?
- try to attract the teacher's attention?
- wait for the teacher to invite you to speak?

2 When you want to interrupt a group of people, do you ...
- wait for a pause in the conversation?
- gesture that you want to say something?
- butt in with what you want to say?

3 When you are listening to someone speaking, do you ...
- make noises and comments as they speak?
- nod and maintain eye contact?
- look away and listen in silence?

4 If there is a long pause in a conversation, do you ...
- feel embarrassed?
- try to fill the silence immediately?
- feel perfectly comfortable?

2 In small groups, compare your answers. What differences would you expect in different cultures?

Listening
Noting the exact words

1 🔲1 Listen to two people discussing cross-cultural differences.
   1 What aspects of cultural behaviour do their two stories illustrate?
   2 How is the behaviour they describe different from what happens in Britain?
   3 What would happen in your culture in these situations?

2 🔲2 Listen to extracts from the conversation. Answer the questions.

Extract A
1 Has Lynne mentioned the seminar before? How do you know?
2 What does Colin say to interrupt?

Extract B
3 How does Colin interrupt to start his story?

Extract C
4 How does Lynne return to her earlier topic?
5 What expression shows that she has forgotten what she was going to say?

Did you notice...?

> You find that the person thinks that ... **you're** trying to stop **them** and interrupt **them**.

> **You** just go up, and **you** say 'Have **you** got a light?' and **they** don't say anything at all.

- Use *you / your* to generalize about what most people do.
- In very formal situations, use *one* and *one's* instead of *you* and *your*.
- *They*, *them*, and *their* can refer to a single indefinite person when their gender is not known.
- A formal alternative is to use *he or she*, *him or her*, and *his or her*.

A	B
clench	your throat
raise	your arms
clear	your eyebrows
fold	your fingers
snap	your fists
raise	your feet
tap	your legs
rub	your head
cross	your eyes
shake	your voice

Pronunciation

1 [3] Listen to some turn-taking expressions and write down the stressed word in each.

2 Listen again and repeat.

Vocabulary
Body language

1 ⏱ **Against the clock!** You have three minutes to match the verbs in column **A** with the nouns in column **B**.

2 What mood or signal, if any, do the actions convey?
You clench your fists when you feel angry or frustrated / to express anger.

3 In pairs, practise miming and guessing the actions in the box below.

tap someone on the shoulder	blow your nose	giggle
beckon someone	sniff	point
pat someone on the back	shrug	stare
nudge someone	wink	frown

4 Are any of these impolite in your country? When?

English in use
Turn-taking

1 ⏱ **Against the clock!** You have two minutes to match a heading to each group of expressions.

Moving on to a new topic   Interrupting
Returning to a topic   Forgetting your point

A	B
Hang on, …	My mind's gone blank.
Sorry, can I just say something?	I've lost my train of thought.
Sorry to interrupt, but …	Where was I?
If I can just make a point please, …	What was I saying?
C	**D**
As I was saying, …	That reminds me of (a friend of
Anyway, going back to (exams), …	mine), …
Anyway, what I was going to	By the way, talking of (football), …
say was, …	Changing the subject completely, …

2 In groups of three, decide on six topics to talk about. Practise speaking, interrupting, and returning to the topic.

Speak out

1 Explain different customs related to some of these topics in your own country or give examples from other cultures you know.

- telephoning
- touching people
- clothes / dressing
- body language and gestures
- birthdays

- punctuality
- weddings
- interrupting
- shopping
- hospitality

2 a Note down five pieces of advice to give to visitors to your country, including one piece of bad advice.

b In groups, take it in turns to speak and identify the bad advice.

Remember

- Practise turn-taking by using different expressions to interrupt and return to a topic.
- Use words and expressions connected with body language.
- Use a range of indefinite pronouns to make generalizations.
- Concentrate on correct sentence stress.

OUR CLEVEREST INVENTION?

In this lesson

- Read quickly to understand the main points of an argument.
- Look at adverbs to express attitude.
- Focus on uses of the definite article.
- Use discourse markers to structure a formal argument.

Speak for yourself

1 How do you prefer to get information, from books or via the Internet? Why?

2 Do you think books will be supplanted by electronic technology? Why / why not?

3 What are the advantages and disadvantages of using books / the Internet?

Reading

Identifying the main arguments

1 Complete these sentences with *the / a book* or *the Internet*.

1 Everyone loves to curl up with _____ .

2 Thanks to _____ , I can access much of the world's great art, literature, and scientific thought within minutes.

3 _____ offers an exciting and invigorating way to disseminate knowledge.

4 _____ is the most potent artefact ever created by humanity.

5 We have a deep emotional attachment to _____ .

6 _____ is a masterpiece of design.

7 For up-to-date knowledge about the state of the world now, use _____ .

2 ☀ **Against the clock!** In two groups, **A** and **B**, **A** read the text below, and **B** turn to the text on *p.104*. You have five minutes to note down the main points that the writers use to support their arguments.

WILL THE BOOK BE SUPPLANTED BY ELECTRONIC TECHNOLOGY?

THE INTERNET

First, can we divorce the sentimentality that surrounds the printed word from this debate? Yes, racks of leather-bound books look fantastic. Yes, everyone loves to curl up with a good book. But the real question is whether the printed word will be able to compete effectively with electronic media as a source of knowledge – and the answer has to be no. On paper, knowledge is restricted and isolated. Once digital, it becomes global, interconnected, collaborative. Often it becomes free.

Thanks to the Internet, I can access much of the world's great art, literature, and scientific thought within minutes, without having to leave my desk. At this moment, volunteers are putting 1,000 of the world's greatest works of literature – from Balzac to Xenephon – into digital form. On a CD-ROM costing tens of pounds, I can access an encyclopedia which once cost hundreds. Surely you can see the benefit of both of these phenomena? And surely you have to believe that for all the aesthetic virtues we associate with the printed page, electronic media offer a much more exciting and invigorating way to disseminate knowledge?

Instead of clinging to the cuddliness of the book, we should be trying to get as many Internet-connected PCs to as many corners of the world as possible. We should save our children from out-of-date textbooks, and get schools connected as quickly as possible. Clearly, those who want to keep their books will do – like those who hang on to vinyl records. But we are looking towards the future here, hopefully a future where knowledge flows freely, ignoring national boundaries or the whims of the publishing industry. Electronic media are vital for this future.

The Guardian

3 Check your ideas with someone in your group.

4 In **A / B** pairs, swap information.

5 Look back at the sentences in **1**. Were your ideas right?

6 **What do you think?** In **A / B** pairs, answer the questions.

   1 Are there any points in the two texts that you disagree with? Why?

   2 Would you rather learn English from a book or on the Internet? Why?

7 Which word or words in *Did you notice ...?* are used ...

   • to agree informally to a request?   • to challenge or convince?

   • to agree formally to a request?   • to state that you are sure?

Vocabulary
Adverbial phrases

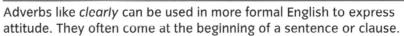
Clearly, those who want to keep their books will do.

Adverbs like *clearly* can be used in more formal English to express attitude. They often come at the beginning of a sentence or clause.

obviously	not surprisingly	fortunately	ironically
sadly	tragically	hopefully	naturally
oddly enough	clearly	surprisingly	understandably
unfortunately	strangely enough	amazingly	predictably

1 In pairs, write three true sentences using these adverbs.

2 Read your sentences to another pair without the adverb. They complete the sentences.

Pronunciation

1 Practise saying these words. Which sound do they have in common?

fortunately	feature
naturally	virtually
future	congratulations
literature	question

2 🔊 Listen and repeat the words.

Language work
Uses of the definite article

> Thanks to **the Internet**, I can access much of **the world's** great art.
>
> *The* is used with nouns that refer to something of which there is only one, or when we know which one is meant, for example:
>
> **a** certain institutions or organizations, e.g. the church, the Internet
>
> **b** geographical or cosmic features, e.g. the sun, the equator
>
> **c** things that people usually have only one of, e.g. the front door, the fridge

1 ☀ **Against the clock!** In pairs, you have two minutes to decide which of the above categories these words could belong to.

- the press
- the council
- the garden
- the roof
- the ground
- the kitchen
- the weather
- the world
- the sky
- the stereo
- the moon
- the car
- the media
- the horizon
- the government

> Usually *the* is not used to make generalizations, e.g.
> I love **books**. (not ~~the books~~)
> **Technology** moves so fast. (not ~~The technology~~)
> In more formal English *the* can be used with a singular countable noun to make generalizations, e.g.
> The invention of **the book** was a milestone in the development of humanity. (= the concept of the book, not a particular book)
> **The mobile phone** has revolutionized communications. (= the concept of the mobile phone, not a particular phone)

2 **What do you think?** Which three inventions are the most beneficial to humanity, and why?
I think the telephone is an important invention because …

English in use
Presenting an argument

Listing points in a speech

First, can we divorce sentimentality from this debate?

Use these discourse markers to move on to a new point.

> First(ly), … second(ly), … third(ly), … and finally, …
> What's more, … In addition to this, …
> Plus the fact that … and on top of that, …

1 Which of these expressions can be used instead of *firstly*?

At first, …   In the first place, …   At the beginning, …   To start with, …
For a start, …   First and foremost, …   First of all, …

2 Which of these expressions can be used instead of *finally*?

Lastly, …   At last, …   In the end, …   Last but not least, …

1  Listen to the intonation of some of the expressions for presenting an argument.

2 Listen again and repeat.

Admitting the truth of an opposing view

Yes, everyone loves to curl up with a good book.

Use these expressions to show you are aware of the other side of the argument.

True, ...   Granted, ...   Admittedly, ...   Yes, ...

3 If someone said, 'Granted, it's handy for sending e-mails ...', are they basically for or against computers?

4 How would you expect the sentence to continue?

Introducing an opinion

It is scarcely surprising that we have a deep emotional attachment to the book. After all, it is the most potent artefact ever created by humanity.

It's scarcely surprising that ...   No wonder ...   After all, ...

5 Which expressions are used to ...?
- state an unsurprising fact • justify an opinion

6 Which word could be used instead of *scarcely*?

7 Complete the sentences using expressions from the boxes in this section.

1 The book has its advantages. _____ , it's cheap and lightweight. _____ , you don't have to install expensive hardware. _____ , you don't need to log on every time you want to find a piece of information.

2 The book will not disappear. _____ , no new technology has entirely supplanted an old one.

3 _____ , the Internet is a godsend if you don't have access to a local library. But many people still prefer to get their information from books.

4 _____ we like to go to bed with a good book. You can't curl up with a computer, after all.

Speak out

In pairs, prepare to give a presentation for or against one topic.
- experiments on animals   • euthanasia   • military service
- choosing the sex of your child   • cloning   • working from home
- the legalization of soft drugs   • body piercing   • banning hand guns

Organize your presentation.
- Give a general introduction, and state your position.
- Concede the opposing arguments.
- List your own arguments with examples and justification.
- Summarize your position with a convincing final sentence.

Follow-up

1 Look again at the texts, and underline all uses of the definite article. See if you can explain why it is used in every case.

2 Find a newspaper article presenting an opinion. Underline and look up the meaning of the discourse markers used.

3 Write a summary of the article.

4 Do a class survey on attitudes to and use of the Internet.

Remember
- Use a range of discourse markers to structure your presentation.
- Use adverbs to express attitude.
- Concentrate on your use of articles.

12
HOW WE MET

In this lesson

- Following narratives.
- Study and practise vocabulary connected with movement and feelings.
- Practise telling stories using appropriate verb forms and expressions.
- Focus on being an active listener.

Speak for yourself

1 In pairs, decide on the four most likely places to meet a partner.

- at a party
- at a supermarket
- on the beach
- at an airport
- at work
- at a disco
- on a train
- in the pub
- at school / university

2 In your country, where else do couples meet?

Listening
Following a narrative

1 These words are from a true story. In pairs, predict what happened.

to stock up	a trolley	the checkout
the ice cream counter	a bunch of flowers	a cheque book
directory enquiries	embarrassed	

2 🔘1 Listen to the whole story.

1 Note down three things you learn about Jane.
2 What happened ...
   - at the ice cream counter?
   - at the checkout?
   - later that day?
   - on their date?

3 🔘2 Listen to another story. Answer the questions.

1 Where does the story start?
2 How was the woman feeling? Why?
3 Where did she first see the man?
4 Where did they next meet?
5 What happened after that?
6 What are the similarities with the story in 2?

Did you notice...?

💬 I thought, 'Well, it's time to go out and stock up on some things.'

💬 I went towards the door thinking 'That's a shame, I'm never going to see him again.'

When telling a story, it is common to report speech or thoughts directly.

Write three examples of what the man in the first story might have thought.

Vocabulary

Feelings and moods

💬 I was a bit **nervous** because you're not really meant to go out on dates with people you've picked up in supermarkets.

💬 She was feeling quite **depressed** because she'd had quite a bad time man-wise recently.

1 In pairs, decide which words / expressions describe positive or negative feelings.

tense	bad-tempered	in good spirits	sorry for yourself
apprehensive	lethargic	restless	dejected
emotional	content	elated	drained
energetic	anxious	fed up	pleased with yourself

2 Complete the sentences with *I was / I was feeling a bit / really* _____ and one of the words / expressions from **1**.

1 ... so I went for a run round the park.
2 ... because I'd just had my manuscript rejected again.
3 ... so I had an early night.
4 ... because it was a beautiful day and I didn't have to work.

3 ✳ **Against the clock!** In pairs, you have four minutes to write three similar half sentences. Test another pair.

Verbs of movement

💬 I was **trundling** around with my trolley.

4 What does *trundle* mean? What other verbs could you use instead?

5 In two groups, **A** and **B**, check these verbs in a dictionary.

A		
rush	crawl	dash
storm	stride	stagger

B		
leap	tiptoe	limp
stroll	wander	march

6 In **A** / **B** pairs, test your partner. Mime or give a definition of the verbs in your box and ask your partner for the verb.

Language work
Narrative verb forms

1 ☀ **Against the clock!** You have four minutes to complete the extract with forms of the verbs in brackets.

> Well, I ¹_____ (go) shopping one day, I ²_____ (live) in East Oxford for about five years, with my two boys, and I ³_____ (have) a boring sort of weekend doing some painting and I ⁴_____ (think), 'Well, it's time to go out and stock up on some things.' Tom ⁵_____ (have) his eighth birthday, so I ⁶_____ (get) some birthday stuff, so I ⁷_____ (set off) to the supermarket. And then I ⁸_____ (trundle) around Sainsbury's with my trolley, when suddenly, this rather interesting-looking man ⁹_____ (appear) at the ice cream counter.

2 🔈 3 Listen to the extract again to check your answers.

3 **Focus on form** Which verb forms are used ...
- to describe events before the story happened?
- to set the scene for the main events of the story?
- for the main events?
- to describe a future event?

4 Try to complete these flashbacks from the story.

> **1** I ... went towards the door thinking, 'Oh, that's a shame, I'm never going to see him again', and then I suddenly realized I was going to see him again because _____ .

> **2** ... and then about eight o'clock that night he telephoned. And it was amazing because _____ so I wasn't in the directory and what he'd done, _____ by looking at my cheque book when I wrote my cheque.

5 🔈 4 Listen and check.

6 Look again at the flashbacks. Are they used ...
- to give a reason for the main event?
- to give information the speaker has not previously mentioned?
- for both reasons?

this and *these*

Use *this* or *these* to introduce a new person or element in the story.
> 💬 *Suddenly* **this** *rather interesting-looking man appeared.*
> 💬 *And there he was with* **these** *flowers.*

7 Complete the sentences with a phrase using *this* or *these*.
1 I was lying by the pool sunbathing, when all of a sudden ...
2 I was driving on the motorway, when ...
3 I was trekking in the rainforest, when suddenly ...
4 I was just about to take a bite of my sandwich, when ...

Fronting with adverbial expressions

We often use fronting devices for dramatic effect in a story. Notice the word order.

💬 ... and then **off I went**.

💬 ... and **there he was** behind me.

8 In pairs, make sentences using these expressions.

and there she stood	and out he leapt	and off I ran
and there they were	so in I marched	

9 Turn to the Tapescript on *p.114*. Listen to Hanne's story again and highlight examples of ...

- how she sets the scene.
- flashbacks or explanations.
- uses of *this* and *these*.
- fronting.
- how she reports her thoughts.

English in use
Being a good listener

  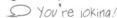

As you are listening, you can help the flow of a story by making comments or noises to show interest and encourage the speaker.

💬 Right ... 💬 Oh no! 💬 You're joking!

1 Turn to the Tapescript on *pp.113/114*. Highlight expressions Hanne uses ...

- to show that she is listening and understanding.
- in response to a surprising or dramatic event.

2 〔0 6〕 Listen to a story, and in the pauses use an expression from **1** to show you are listening.

Speak out

1 Plan the story of how you or someone you know met a partner.

2 In pairs, tell your stories. Make suggestions about how to improve each other's storytelling.

3 In groups of three or four, retell your stories.

> **Follow-up**
>
> **1** Ask other English speakers that you know how they met their partner or a friend.
>
> **2** Look up the use of the past perfect in a grammar reference book. Note down two things you learn.
>
> **3** Practise telling the story of a famous meeting in a film or novel, as you would if you were telling a friend. Set the scene carefully, and use flashbacks.
>
> **4** Use a dictionary to research different ways of looking, e.g. *gaze*, *glance*, and write these in a new page in your vocabulary book.

Remember

- Use appropriate narrative verb forms to tell stories.
- Use *this* and *these* and fronting expressions for dramatic effect.
- Use a range of verbs of movement and adjectives to describe feelings.
- Show interest by commenting and helping the story along.

13 HOW CAN I PUT THIS?

In this lesson

- Practise using English in different social situations.
- Focus on how to prepare people for difficult news.
- Study and practise verbs and adverbs for reporting conversations.

Pronunciation

1 ◉3 Listen to the intonation patterns of some expressions which prepare the way for difficult news.

2 Listen again and repeat.

Speak for yourself

1 In pairs, choose two of these situations and improvise conversations.
- Offer to help a flatmate before a party.
- Apologize to a friend for losing a book he / she lent you.
- Invite a friend to do something with you this evening.
- Ask a colleague to cover for you while you have an afternoon off.

2 Listen to a different pair's conversations.

Listening
What's going on?

1 ◉1 Listen to eight short conversations. Match one or more of the verbs from the box to each conversation.

accuse	offer	turn down	arrange	accept	refuse	agree
apologize	admit	invite	deny	request	suggest	

2 ◉ **Against the clock!** In pairs, you have four minutes to report the content of the conversations, using the appropriate verbs.

3 Listen again to check your ideas.

4 Look at the Tapescript on *p.114*. Underline any interesting new words and expressions.

English in use
Preparing the way for difficult news

1 In pairs, choose three of these opening phrases and make dialogues.
1 Could I ask you a big favour?
2 You know I said I could lend you my car this weekend ...?
3 Have you got a moment?
4 I've got a bit of a problem ...
5 You know that book you lent me?
6 I don't quite know how to put this, but ...
7 There's something I've been meaning to tell you.
8 I'm afraid I've got an apology to make ...

2 ◉2 Listen and compare your ideas with the dialogues on the tape.

3 Do you use similar openers in your language?

Vocabulary
Verb patterns

1 ⏱ **Against the clock!** In teams, you have five minutes to decide which sentences are incorrect and correct them.

1 She promised **me to write** every day.
2 He admitted **to forging** my signature.
3 He suggested **me to take up** yoga.
4 She pleaded **with me not to tell** her father.
5 She swore **to tell** the truth.
6 He recommended **that I should see** an optician.
7 He confessed **cheating** in the exam.
8 She told me off **for borrowing** her bike without asking.
9 He owned up **for stealing** the video.
10 They urged **me to get** a second opinion.

Verb / adverb collocations

Did you notice...?

1 In which two of the sentences in **2** does the adverb comes after the verb?
2 Write two more sentences using the two verb / adverb collocations.

2 Complete the sentences with an adverb from the box. In some cases, more than one is possible.

| willingly | categorically | freely | warmly | faithfully |
| kindly | reluctantly | strongly | flatly | profusely |

1 My colleagues _____ congratulated me on my promotion.
2 James apologized _____ for losing his temper.
3 My bank _____ denied having received the cheque in the post.
4 I _____ admit that I lied about my age to get the job.
5 The company _____ refused to pay me a relocation allowance.
6 Jonny _____ offered to cook me dinner last night.
7 All my friends _____ advised me to seek legal advice.
8 I promised _____ to pay my brother back within a week.
9 The injured player _____ accepted my offer of help.
10 Steve _____ agreed to work overtime but he really didn't want to.

3 In **A** / **B** pairs. **A** close your book. **B** give a reporting verb from **2** and ask for a collocating adverb.

Speak out

1 In groups of three, **A** and **B** choose a reporting verb from this unit. Describe a recent experience and use the verb.
C monitor the language for accuracy. Swap roles.

2 In new groups of three, **A** and **B** improvise the conversations in *Speak for yourself* again, and **C** monitor. Swap roles.

Remember

• Use a variety of functional language from this unit.
• Use expressions to prepare the way for difficult news.
• Use a range of reporting verbs and verb / adverb collocations.
• Concentrate on using appropriate intonation patterns.

14
WE'VE BEEN HAD

In this lesson

- Read quickly to find specific information.
- Practise asking for and providing clarification.
- Focus on expressions connected with telling lies.
- Look at proverbs.

Speak for yourself

1 Write down four things you associate with New York.

2 In pairs, compare your ideas.

3 What impressions do you have of New Yorkers?

4 Have you ever been there? If not, would you like to go? Why / why not?

Reading
Following a newspaper story

1 Look at the photo, the map, and the headline of the article. In pairs, think of things you would like to know.
I wonder how long it took him.
I wonder if he could speak any English.

2 ⏱ **Against the clock!** You have three minutes to read the article and try to find answers to your questions.

BOY IN **4,500-MILE** TREK
TO FIND HIS FATHER

Edwin Daniel Sabillon, a slight 13-year-old boy who arrived in New York on Saturday with only a change of clothes, a paper bag containing $24, three biscuits, and his birth certificate, wanted so badly to find the father he had only ever seen in snapshots that he travelled 4,500 miles from Honduras to find him. Over 37 days he rode buses and trucks, walked, cycled, and hitchhiked, often through dangerous territory. In spite of hunger, the loss of his wallet containing his father's phone number, and the fact that he speaks no English at all, he was carried along by luck, and the charity of strangers.

The epic journey began after Hurricane Mitch tore through Honduras, destroying his home and killing his mother, his brother, and his grandfather. The boy wrote to the father he knew was living in New York, and several months later, a letter came back with $200 and an arrangement for a roadside rendezvous. It seemed **a little haphazard**, but Edwin was determined to make the meeting. His father said he would be waiting at the entrance to La Guardia Airport on three successive days, 25, 26, and 27 June, wearing a white shirt and black hat.

And so, on 22 May, Edwin waved goodbye to his friends in the village of San Francisco de Yojoa Cortez, and headed north on a trek that took him through Guatemala and up the east coast of Mexico to the edge of the United States. He then continued via Houston, New Orleans, and **inexplicably** – Edwin's geography appears to have failed him at this point – down to Miami, Florida, where he managed to beg money for the bus journey to New York.

Sunday morning found the young boy at a bus terminal in Upper Manhattan. For a while, he strolled unfamiliar streets, and then made his way to the airport just as any New Yorker would – by hailing a taxi. But when he got there, there was no sign of Edwin's father. So the taxi driver, 35-year-old José Basora, took pity on Edwin and drove him to his home in the Bronx, before alerting the police to **the boy's plight**.

'We'll do the best that we can to try and help him,' promised Mayor Rudolph Giuliani, indicating that the authorities will **turn a blind eye to** the illegalities of the boy's entry into the United States. And now Edwin, who is in city **foster care**, can only wait and hope that his father shows up.

The Independent

Did you notice…?

- 💬 I **honestly** believed he made that journey.
- 💬 I feel disappointed, **to be honest with you.**
- 💬 I think we've got all our values upside down, **to tell you the truth.**
- 💬 I **genuinely** believed him.

Which expressions would you use …

1 to insist that you are being sincere?
2 to give a slightly negative opinion?

3 What is your reaction to the story? Does anything surprise you?

4 In pairs, decide what the expressions in **bold** mean.

Listening
A radio broadcast

1 🔊1 Listen to **Part 1** of a news programme broadcast the day after the story of Edwin broke in the newspapers.
   1 What do the words 'We've been had' mean?
   2 What do you think of Officer Granger's reaction?

2 Listen to **Part 2**. Note down whether the five people interviewed approve or disapprove of what Edwin did. Who do you agree with?

3 Listen to **Parts 1** and **2** of the broadcast again. Decide what these idiomatic expressions mean.

   1 Edwin was **telling a tall tale**.
   2 You can't **take anyone at their word** nowadays.
   3 Now he's going to **get away with it**.
   4 **They've got egg on their faces**.
   5 There's a **silver lining** for us there.
   6 He **took us all for a ride**.

4 **What do you think?** In pairs, answer the questions.
   1 Were you taken in by Edwin's story when you read the article?
   2 Have your impressions of New York and New Yorkers changed?

Vocabulary
Expressions connected with telling lies

1 In pairs, look at the expressions. What's the difference between them?

1	He made out he was English.	5	I was taken in.
2	He was economical with the truth.	6	He was having me on.
3	He was kidding.	7	He told a white lie.
4	It was a hoax.	8	He was pulling my leg.

Proverbs

> So I guess there's a **silver lining** for us there.

This refers to the proverb *Every cloud has a silver lining*.

It is common to use part of a proverb rather than quoting it in full.

2 What do the half-proverbs in **bold** mean?

1 I don't usually eat so late but we are on holiday and **when in Rome** …

2 She said her exams went well but she shouldn't **count her chickens** just yet.

3 I wish he wouldn't spend all his time in the office. You know what they say about **all work and no play** …

4 The whole team is incompetent. It's a clear case of **too many cooks**.

5 I don't know what she sees in Jack. Oh well, **it takes all sorts**, I suppose.

3 Complete these proverbs with the words in the box.

eating	never	mind	fonder	speed	cure

1 Out of sight, out of _____ .
2 More haste, less _____ .
3 Better late than _____ .
4 Prevention is better than _____ .
5 The proof of the pudding is in the _____ .
6 Absence makes the heart grow _____ .

4 In pairs, think of situations in which you might use some of the proverbs in **2** and **3**.

English in use
Asking for and providing clarification

1  Listen to someone talking about a man who lied every day.

1 What did he lie about?

2 Why did he lie?

3 What happened in the end?

Pronunciation

1 ⊙3 Listen to seven examples of asking for and providing clarification. Write down the stressed word / words in each.

2 Listen again, check, and repeat.

2 Listen again and tick (✓) the expressions used to ask for clarification.

Asking for clarification	Providing clarification
So hang on, ...	Yes, exactly. / Yes, that's right.
What, you mean, ...	Not exactly ...
What, so ...	No, not at all ...
So, are you saying ...	

3 In **A** / **B** pairs, ask for and provide clarification.
- Explain how and why you decided to enrol for this language course.
- Tell the story of Edwin Sabillon or another story you've heard on the news.

Speak out

1 In pairs, look at these situations. Would you tell the truth?

1 Your friend has his hair cut in a style that you don't think suits him. He asks you for your opinion. What do you say?

2 You are asked to provide a job reference for a friend who is not very punctual and a bit lazy. What do you write?

3 You oversleep and are half an hour late for work. What do you tell your boss?

4 You go out for a drink with an old boyfriend / girlfriend. Do you tell your present boyfriend / girlfriend?

5 You are undercharged at a restaurant. Do you tell the waiter?

6 You accept an exciting invitation even though you have a prior engagement with someone else. Do you confess when you cancel the first arrangement?

7 An eight-year-old asks you if Santa Claus really exists. What do you say?

8 You know that a friend's husband is having an affair. Do you tell her?

Remember
- Use different expressions to talk about telling lies.
- Ask for and provide clarification.
- Concentrate on correct sentence stress.

2 a Make notes on one of the following situations and prepare to tell a short story. Include one false detail.
- an eventful journey you have made
- a time when you had to tell a lie
- a time when you were taken in
- a time when someone lied to you

b In groups of three, tell your story. As you listen to the other stories, ask for clarification and at the end, guess which detail was false.

Follow-up
1 Write about a time when you were taken in, or when you took someone in.

2 Practise asking for clarification next time you have a conversation in English.

3 Translate some proverbs from your country into English and put them on a poster to display in the classroom.

4 Go through a newspaper article and underline any useful idiomatic or multi-word expressions you find. Add them to your vocabulary notebook.

Speak for yourself

1 Tell other people about a car you own or would like to have.

2 Which of these statements best sums up your attitude to cars? In pairs, explain why.
- My car is an essential part of my life.
- My car comes in handy but I could manage without it.
- I really wish I had a car.
- I may have a car one day, but I don't need one at the moment.
- I never intend to own a car.

Listening
Note-taking from a speech

1 You are going to hear two people making speeches for and against the car. What arguments do you think each speaker will put forward?

2 **○1** In two groups, **A** and **B**, **A** listen to the argument for and **B** to the argument against. Make notes for each of these topics.
- pollution • congestion • health care
- public transport • road-building

3 In **A** / **B** pairs, exchange information.

4 **What do you think?** In pairs, answer the questions.
1 Are there any points you disagree with?
2 Do you agree or disagree that the car does more harm than good?

Pronunciation

1 **○2** Listen to this statement and mark whether the speaker's voice rises or falls on the underlined words.

Cars are <u>noisy</u>, they are <u>smelly</u>, and they are <u>dangerous</u>.

2 Predict the rises and falls in these statements.
1 They clog up the streets, they emit fumes, and they cause accidents.
2 People like them, they've got used to having them, and they're not going to give them up.
3 They bring in revenue from car tax, road tax, and tax on fuel.

3 **○3** Listen and check.

4 Listen again and repeat the sentences.

Did you notice...?

💬 *As for congestion, well this could easily be solved ...*

To introduce a new point in a speech, use expressions like *As for ...* , *With regard to ...* , *Turning now to ...* .

Turn to the Tapescript on *pp.115/116* and underline expressions used to introduce a new point.

Vocabulary
Verb / noun collocations

1 Which verbs were used with the nouns in **bold** in the two speeches?

The car _____ a major **threat** to our planet.

Public transport cannot _____ everyone's **needs**.

Instead of _____ **war** on cars, we need to accommodate them.

2 Turn to the Tapescript on *pp.115/116* and check.

3 ☀ **Against the clock!** You have three minutes to match the verbs on the left with a group of nouns on the right.

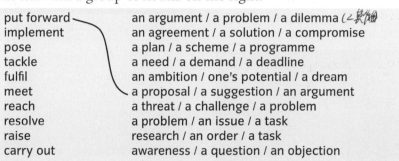

put forward	an argument / a problem / a dilemma (之長拥)
implement	an agreement / a solution / a compromise
pose	a plan / a scheme / a programme
tackle	a need / a demand / a deadline
fulfil	an ambition / one's potential / a dream
meet	a proposal / a suggestion / an argument
reach	a threat / a challenge / a problem
resolve	a problem / an issue / a task
raise	research / an order / a task
carry out	awareness / a question / an objection

4 Look at the box again for one minute. Test your partner. Read out a verb and ask for some of the collocating nouns. Swap roles.

Language work
Putting forward proposals

Use a clause with *should* ...

- after *suggest*, *propose*, and *recommend*
- to express the concept of necessity or importance.

We are proposing that **traffic should be restricted** in the rush hour.
She suggested that **we should try** to reach a compromise.
It's absolutely vital that **we should meet** this challenge.
It is essential that **we should tackle** the problem of pollution.

Use *should*, *shouldn't*, or *need to* to give your opinion

We need to come up with radical solutions.
The government should be trying to address the problem.
We shouldn't close our eyes to the problem.

In pairs, discuss these questions in relation to three of the issues below.

1 What proposals have been made in your country?

2 What do you think should be done?

- road accidents
- global warming
- air pollution
- motorways
- road rage
- taxation

Pronunciation

1 Listen to the stress and intonation of expressions for making your point.

2 ⊙ 4 Listen again and repeat the expressions.

English in use
Making your point

Phrases to state a fact or opinion

💬 *The simple fact of the matter is, the car is here to stay.*

The fact is, ...	What we've got to remember is ...
There is no doubt that ...	Quite frankly, ...
It seems to me that ...	Quite honestly, ...

Sentences with *what*

💬 *What we should be doing is using public transport more.*

1 Match the two parts of the sentences.

1 What we need to do ...
2 What we want ...
3 What we mustn't do ...
4 What has grown ...
5 What worries me ...
6 What we should be doing ...
7 What will happen ..⟨⟩
8 What is being proposed ...

a ... is that congestion will be reduced.
b ... is that people might be discouraged from using public transport.
c ... is cutting the cost of public transport.
d ... is encourage more people to use buses.
e ... is cleaner air.
f ... is that parking charges should be increased.
g ... is increase air pollution.
h ... is the number of cars on the roads.

The use of *simply* for emphasis

💬 *... it's simply not fair to put the blame on cars.*

2 Where could you put *simply* in these sentences?

1 It's not true that cars clog up city centres.
2 We won't solve the problem by declaring war on the bus.
3 We can't put people's lives at risk because there isn't enough money.
4 Travelling by bus is not attractive.
5 If fares are too high, people won't use public transport.
6 The problem is that there aren't enough roads.

3 In pairs, look at the photos and give your opinion using the language on this page.

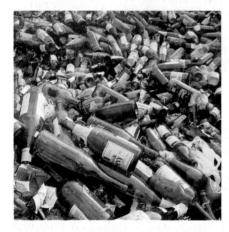

Speak out

1 a You are going to take part in a debate on how to solve the traffic problems of a large city. In three groups, **A**, **B**, and **C**, read your proposals below. Prepare to argue for your proposal with the rest of your group. Make notes on ...

* the advantages of the proposal.
* how the scheme will be financed and how it will work in practice.
* how to defend possible criticisms of the proposal.

b In **A** / **B** / **C** groups, present and discuss your proposals and try to reach agreement.

2 In groups, discuss traffic problems and solutions in your city.

A

* Ban private cars from the city centre (completely or at certain times).
* Introduce tolls on major roads into the city centre.
* Introduce a park-and-ride scheme (motorists park on the outskirts of the city and take buses in).
* Introduce traffic-calming measures (speed bumps and speed restrictions).
* Pay a yearly bonus to non-car owners.

B

* Build a ring road around the city.
* Provide more car-parking spaces and underground car parks.
* Widen roads in the city, and build more flyovers and underground roads.
* Increase parking charges in the city.
* Subsidize and encourage the use of zero-emission cars.

C

* Increase public transport provision.
* Subsidize buses to make them cheap or free at certain times.
* Build more bus lanes and cycle lanes.
* Introduce trams and shared car schemes.
* Implement an education programme on transport and pollution.

Follow-up

1 Write a report of the debate.

2 Study the Tapescript on *pp.115/116* and make a note of new words or expressions, especially those used to make a point strongly.

3 Prepare to give a short oral presentation on how to solve a problem connected with your country, city, school, or university.

4 Look in a dictionary to find examples of how the verb / noun collocations on *p.51* are used. Write sentences of your own in your vocabulary book.

16
WHAT ARE YOUR PLANS?

In this lesson

- Talk and ask about plans.
- Study and practise expressions connected with plans, activity, and inactivity.
- Focus on multi-word verbs connected with changes of plan.

TUE	Salsa
WED	London / party 9pm
THU	Mum and Dad – dinner?
FRI	Ten-pin bowling
SAT	Cricket
SUN	Trip to Bath?

Speak for yourself

⏱ **Against the clock!** In pairs, you have two minutes to decide how you would tell someone about these plans in your diary.

Listening
Noting the exact words

1 [◉1] Listen to eight people discussing their weekend plans. Which sound the most interesting to you?

2 Listen to conversations **1** and **2** again. Complete the extracts.

1

I think on Friday night I _____ .

I _____ to Nottingham to visit some friends up there, and I _____ stay the night, have a meal and _____ the next day.

So _____ on Saturday?

Yes, yeah, yeah, 'cos I _____ on Saturday night.

2

Well, pretty much the same plans as every weekend, I _____ one day.

I _____ a lazy weekend. I _____ , sorting out things ...

---

3 Listen to conversations **3** and **4** again. Note down useful expressions.

Pronunciation

1 [◉2] Listen to these extracts. Notice the pronunciation of *going* and *going to*.

2 In which extracts did you hear the pronunciation /ˈɡʌnə/?

3 How do you feel about using this pronunciation yourself?

4 Which word was stressed most strongly in sentence **7**? Why?

id you notice...?

💬 *I'll probably go to the gym.*

Shall, *'ll*, and *won't* can be used to express your spontaneous plans or predictions for the future and are usually qualified with *I don't think*, *I probably*, etc.

I don't think I'll stay for coffee.
I probably won't stay up very late.
I think I shall just crash out.
I'll definitely have an early night.
Perhaps I'll pop round a bit later.

Use the expressions to make spontaneous plans for the rest of the day.

English in use
Talking about plans

1 Look at the different ways of talking about your plans. Match a heading to categories 1 to 5.

Asking questions about plans	Expressing a fixed plan / arrangement
Distancing yourself from a plan	Expressing a plan that is not fixed
Talking about a changed plan	

1 _____
   I was going to ...
   I had been hoping to ...

2 _____
   I'm going to be _____ ing ...
   I'll be _____ ing ...

3 _____
   I'm thinking of _____ ing ...
   I might ...

4 _____
   What are you doing ...?
   Have you got any plans for ...?
   Have you got anything lined up for ...?

5 _____
   I'm going to ...
   I've got a ...
   I've arranged to ...
   I'm _____ ing ...

2 In pairs, ask and answer about your plans for the weekend.

Vocabulary
Activity, inactivity, and changes of plan

1 ◉ **Against the clock!** In pairs, you have four minutes to complete these colloquial expressions with appropriate words.

1 I think on Sunday I shall just **crash** _____ and have an early night.
2 I'm going to **have a lie-**_____ on Sunday.
3 I'm _____ **to my eyes** in work today but I'm _____ **a loose end** tomorrow.
4 I'm **tied** _____ all this week, with meetings and that kind of thing.
5 I'm just going to watch TV when I get in tonight. I really need to **wind** _____ .
6 I'd love to go with you but I'm a bit **pushed** _____ **time** this weekend.
7 On Friday night I intend to **put my feet** _____ and take it easy.
8 I was hoping to go away this weekend but I'm **snowed** _____ with work.

2 Which expressions in **1** describe activity and which inactivity?

3 In pairs, check the meaning of these multi-word verbs in a dictionary and find an example sentence. Make true sentences of your own.

> call off   talk someone out of   go through with   fall through
> bring forward   get out of   pull out   stick with

Remember
• Use a range of expressions to talk about your plans.
• Use colloquial expressions and multi-word verbs.
• Concentrate on the pronunciation of *going to*.

Speak out

1 Move round the class asking about other people's plans. Use some of these time expressions. Decide on three things to do with a friend.

• at lunch time   • in the break   • this evening
• tomorrow evening   • in the summer   • the weekend after next

2 In pairs, describe the three things you are going to do.

17
AWAY FROM IT ALL

In this lesson

- Read to understand the key points of a text.
- Focus on compound nouns and two-part expressions.
- Practise talking about change.
- Practise describing places.

Speak for yourself

1 In which of these places ...
- do you live now?
- would you like to be living now?
- would you like to bring up a family?
- would you like to live when you retire?

in the heart of a big city	in the suburbs	on the outskirts of a city
in a small town	in a village	in the countryside

2 If you had to move away from the place where you live now, what would you miss? What would you be glad to leave behind?

Reading
Finding key points

1 Do these words / expressions refer to the town or the country?

peace and quiet hustle and bustle the green belt exhaust fumes	
thatched cottages a sense of community the frantic pace of life	
squalor wildlife isolation hedgerows green space	

2 In two groups, **A** read **Text A** on *p.57* and **B** turn to *p.105*. Check your ideas.

3 ☀ **Against the clock!** You have three minutes to answer these questions with a partner who has read the same text.

   1 Where does the writer live now?

   2 Does she prefer the town or the countryside?

WE moved to a crumbling mansion block in central London when my youngest child was five. Our Cambridge friends were aghast. How could we possibly give up green space on our doorstep, the neighbourhood school, the safe environment, for crowds, congestion, and urban squalor? But with two of us working in the metropolis, we felt we had no choice.

It didn't take long for us to convert. Indeed, in ten years I've become a hard-line metropolitan. I've become allergic to the countryside I grew up in. The sight of an idyllic thatched cottage or a picturesque village green now fills me with dread. They remind me of the grim drive to the out-of-town superstore for groceries, the endless hanging about, the lawn always needing to be mowed, and the neighbours complaining when bored youngsters kicked their ball too close to their greenhouse.

To live in the centre of a city is to be permanently intoxicated with the speed of it all – it's like being in a perpetual state of fast-forward. I swear that nowadays it's the frantic pace of city life that makes me think straight and stick to the point in a conversation. Some of my best ideas are produced in an advanced state of stress, under the pressure of having struggled to meet a deadline, or arrive on time at a lecture hall or studio, through impossible traffic. And one of the surprises of city life is the lack of isolation. I've discovered that the neighbours on my staircase are as committed to the local community as the inhabitants of any sleepy village in the country.

Besides, the more of us who can be persuaded back into high density living in the city's hurly-burly, the more green space that will be freed up, out there in the country's green belt. So that the generations of country lovers will be able to continue their love affair with all that grass. Personally, I much prefer the view from my roof terrace, from where I can drink in the impossible noise, and watch the endless comings and goings, the hustle and bustle, and the thrill of inner-London life in the new millennium.

The Guardian

4 Note down positive and negative features of the town and the countryside from the texts. Compare ideas with your partner.

5 Highlight three new words / phrases in your text that you would like to understand. With your partner, try to guess the meanings from context. Check your ideas in a dictionary.

6 In **A / B** pairs, exchange information about your texts.

7 **What do you think?** In small groups, discuss the questions with reference to both texts.

   1 In what ways are the descriptions of the town and the countryside in Britain similar to what you would find in your country? How are they different?

   2 Have the texts made you think about the town or country in a new way?

Vocabulary
Adjectives for the countryside

💬 ... a picturesque village green ...

1 Which adjectives could describe the landscapes in the photos?

flat	picturesque	hilly	lush	wild
gentle	rugged	bleak	fertile	tame
mountainous	spectacular	barren	rocky	arid

2 Describe different landscapes in your country using the adjectives.

Compound nouns for towns

1 Match words in column **A** with words in column **B** to make compound nouns.

A	B		A	B
car	block		town	crossing
concert	complex		housing	dump
pedestrian	corner		parking	arcade
tower	hall		bus	hall
road	park		corner	estate
street	precinct		amusement	meter
leisure	mall		rubbish	shop
shopping	works		pedestrian	stop

2 Which of these can you find near your home?

3 Which three are most important to a town?

4 ⏱ **Against the clock!** You have three minutes to look again at your texts on *p.57* and *p.105* and find more compound nouns.

Language work
Two-part expressions

💬 I can watch the endless **comings and goings**, the **hustle and bustle**, and the **thrill** of inner–London life.

1 Complete the sentences. Check in a dictionary if necessary.
   1 Eventually, by **trial and** _____ , he found the correct combination.
   2 This booklet supplies all the **facts and** _____ about global warming.
   3 There are certain important **rules and** _____ that must be followed.
   4 Having a massage is an excellent way of relieving **aches and** _____ .
   5 This book contains over a hundred **tried and** _____ recipes.
   6 The insurance policy does not cover **wear and** _____ to the equipment.
   7 Successful negotiation involves a certain amount of **give and** _____ .
   8 Terry's vintage Ford Cabriolet was his **pride and** _____ .
   9 I'm **sick and** _____ of receiving so much junk mail.
   10 They were relieved when the children turned up **safe and** _____ .

2 In pairs, explain what the expressions mean in your own words.

3 Test your partner. Give the first word of some of the two-part expressions and ask for the second. Swap roles.

English in use
Talking about change

The countryside **isn't natural any more**.
The city streets **are no longer safe**.
Birds **used to sing** in the hedgerows.
The beaches **never used to be** polluted.
There **didn't use to be** a ring road around the town.
Whole forests **have been chopped down**.
The dance hall **has been turned into** a cinema.
They've built a housing estate on the outskirts of town.
They've knocked down the old theatre and built a multi-storey car park.

1 Which of the statements above are true of where you live?

2 In pairs, **A** and **B**, **A** turn to *p.105* and **B** to *p.108*. Describe your pictures and discuss how the places have changed, using the expressions in **1**.

Speak out

1 a Think of a place you know well and how it has changed. Make notes.

b In groups of three, describe your place.

c **What do you think?** Answer the questions.
  1 Is the countryside changing for the better or the worse?
  2 What could be done to preserve the countryside in your country?

2 a Think of the place where you would most like to spend a day. Make notes in answer to the questions
  • Why have you chosen to go there?
  • What season and time of day is it?
  • What can you see, hear, and smell?
  • How will you spend the day?
  • How do you feel?

b In groups of three, take it in turns to talk about your places and what you would do there.

c Decide which of the three places you would rather go to, and why.

Follow-up

1 Interview someone about whether they would prefer to live in the town or the country, and why.

2 Prepare to give a short oral report on the countryside in your country, or another country you know. Talk about …
  • the types of landscape, and geographical features.
  • who lives in the countryside and what they do.
  • how the countryside is used for leisure pursuits.

3 Start a page in your vocabulary notebook for compound nouns and add eight new ones.

4 Write a paragraph about the town or village where you live, and the advantages and disadvantages of living there.

Speak for yourself

1 Read the following extracts about Martians (men), and Venusians (women). Make notes on ...

- what Martians or Venusians value.
- how they like to view themselves.
- how they cope with problems.

MARTIANS value power, competency, efficiency, and achievement. They fantasize about powerful cars, faster computers, gadgets and new, more powerful technology. They are concerned with outdoor activities, like hunting, fishing, and racing cars, and are more interested in objects and things than in people and feelings. Martians pride themselves on doing things all by themselves, since asking for help when you can do things yourself is perceived as a sign of weakness. Hence they will keep their problems to themselves unless they require help from another person to find a solution. When they get upset, they prefer not to burden their friends with what is bothering them, and instead retreat to their caves to mull over their problems. If they can't find a solution, they do something to relax and disengage their mind; or they engage in something more challenging like racing a car, competing in a contest, or climbing a mountain.

VENUSIANS value love, beauty, and relationships. They find fulfilment through supporting and nurturing each other, and their sense of self is defined through sharing and the quality of their relationships. Rather than building highways and tall buildings, they are more concerned with living together in harmony, community, and loving co-operation. Communication is of primary importance, and sharing their feelings is much more important than achieving goals and success. They pride themselves on being intuitive, and considerate of the feelings of others. When Venusians feel upset, or overwhelmed by feelings of stress, confusion, or hopelessness, they find relief by sharing their problems with friends and talking them over in detail.

Men are from Mars, Women are from Venus

2 What do you think? Do you agree with the points made in the extracts?

Did you notice...?

These expressions from the conversation are used to give examples.

💬 *If I take an example from my own family, I have ...*

💬 *For example, I would always send ...*

💬 *Let me take the example of a friend of mine, who ...*

💬 *If you look at Princess Diana, for example, she ...*

💬 *In some cases, you could cite Mrs Thatcher as an example, they ...*

Which of these expressions do you normally use?

Listening
Following a discussion

1 🔲 Listen to four extracts from a conversation between Jane and Nick about gender differences. Choose the best heading for each extract.

Men and women in the workplace   Nature versus nurture
Bringing up boys and girls   Differences between men and women

2 Choose an extract, listen again, and answer the questions.

Extract A

1 Who thinks character is ...
- genetically determined?
- determined by upbringing?

Extract B

2 Note down the examples the speakers use to illustrate ...
- the ways boys and girls are treated differently.
- how boys and girls differ by nature.

Extract C

3 Why does Nick send his wife to the garage, but fix shelves himself ?
4 What does the example of Princess Diana illustrate about men and women?

Extract D

5 What are the two points of disagreement between Nick and Jane?

3 **What do you think?** Which opinions from the conversation do you agree or disagree with?

Vocabulary
Personal characteristics

💬 *I have an elder sister who's very very ambitious, very very career-orientated, very very determined, quite materialistic in fact.*

1 ☀ **Against the clock!** In two groups, **A** and **B**, you have three minutes to decide whether the words in your box are positive, negative, or both, depending on the context.

2 Check your ideas in a dictionary.

3 In **A / B** pairs, test your partner. Choose a word from your box and ask for a definition or an example sentence.

A			
thick-skinned	self-effacing	career-orientated	considerate
single-minded	down-to-earth	intuitive	aggressive
conscientious	sullen	decisive	sensitive

B			
ruthless	caring	determined	impulsive
obstinate	self-sufficient	materialistic	status-conscious
cautious	stand-offish	ambitious	well-balanced

4 In pairs, choose five adjectives that you usually associate with men and five with women.

Language work
Similarities and differences

1 **Focus on form** In pairs, answer the questions.

  1 Which words from the box could you use to complete the sentences?

  • Men are _____ more aggressive than women.

  • Women are _____ as aggressive as men.

much	just	not	far
nothing like	considerably	slightly	infinitely
a bit	a lot	nowhere near	marginally

  2 Decide on one word to complete the sentences.

  • Men's priorities are totally different _____ / similar _____ / exactly the same _____ / identical _____ women's.

  • _____ comparison with women, men are very single-minded.

  • Compared _____ men, women tend to be family-orientated.

  • Women talk about their feelings, _____ men talk about football.

  • There's no difference _____ men's and women's personalities.

2 Use the expressions in **1** to compare yourself with your family.

3 Decide on differences in character between men and women, using adjectives from *p.61*.

Modifying expressions

In general, ...	In my experience, ...	In some parts of the world, ...
As a rule, ...	To a certain extent, ...	In the eyes of the law, ...
On average, ...	In theory, ...	In the past, ...
In many jobs, ...	In some households, ...	Traditionally, ...

... because of their upbringing.
... by nature.
... but it really depends on the individual.

4 How far do you agree with these statements? Change them where necessary, using modifying expressions from the box.

  1 Women do far more housework than men.
  2 Men are the main breadwinners.
  3 Women have exactly the same rights as men.
  4 Men aren't as intuitive as women.
  5 Women are infinitely better at looking after children.
  6 Men are more career-orientated than women.
  7 Women live slightly longer than men.
  8 Men have better spatial awareness.
  9 Women are more articulate in talking about their feelings.
  10 Women are nothing like as interested in computers as men.
  11 Girls like playing with dolls, whereas boys like playing with guns.
  12 Women wear the trousers.

5 Talk about other differences between men and women, including the things they like doing, are good at, and talk about.

Pronunciation

1 [○2] Listen to ten statements and write down the stressed words in each.

2 What is the pronunciation of *than*, *as*, and *are*?

3 Practise repeating the sentences.

English in use
Agreeing, disagreeing, and half agreeing

1 ☀ **Against the clock!** You have three minutes to list the expressions in the box under one of the three headings.

Agreeing   Disagreeing   Half agreeing

1 You're absolutely right.	8 That's rubbish!
2 I don't think that's true.	9 I see what you mean, but …
3 I disagree, I'm afraid.	10 That's true in a way, but …
4 I take your point, but …	11 That's right.
5 Absolutely.	12 Well, it depends.
6 Come on!	13 To a certain extent, but …
7 Do you really think so?	14 I would agree with that.

2 Which two expressions would you probably only use with people you know well?

Speak out

1 Rate your opinion for each statement.

agree	1	2	3	4	5	disagree

☐ There is a 'glass ceiling' that stops women rising to top level jobs.

☐ If a working couple have children, the woman should stay at home to look after them.

☐ Sexual harassment in the workplace is a big problem for women in my country.

☐ Parents should bring up boys and girls in exactly the same way.

☐ Women make better bosses than men.

☐ Young women nowadays have more choices than men.

2 In groups, choose three of the statements and compare opinions.

Follow-up

1 With another person, discuss similarities and differences between you and members of your family or friends.

2 Start a page in your vocabulary book for personal characteristics and add eight new words from this lesson.

3 Listen to or watch a discussion programme in English and notice the language used.

Speak for yourself

Think about your most recent holiday. In pairs, talk about ...

- the journey
- the accommodation
- the food
- people you met
- the weather
- what you did

Listening
Following two anecdotes

1 In pairs, look at the cartoons and decide what happened.

2 🔊1 Listen to anecdotes **A** and **B**. Were your predictions right?

3 Listen again and make notes for both anecdotes using the headings.

Where it happened   What exactly happened
When it happened   Adjectives used

4 Turn to the Tapescript on *p.117* and highlight expressions used to ...
- start an anecdote
- finish an anecdote
- start a new anecdote

5 Add details to anecdotes **A** and **B** by completing these sentences.

A
The people having their lunch ...
The woman sitting at the table next to me ...
The woman serving the drinks ...

B
The friend sitting in front of me ...
The friend driving ...
A man walking down the slope ...

Did you notice...?

Relative clauses containing participles are often shortened in spoken English.

💬 The bar was full of *people having their lunch* ...

(not *people who were having* ...)

💬 The *friend driving* realized and stopped ...

(not *the friend who was driving* ...)

Vocabulary
Collocations

💬 ... it was **freezing cold**, **pitch black**, couldn't see a thing ...

1 ☀ **Against the clock!** You have three minutes to match the words below to make extreme descriptions.

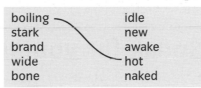

boiling	idle
stark	new
brand	awake
wide	hot
bone	naked

bone	open
fast	dry
soaking	cold
stone	asleep
wide	wet

2 Which of the expressions could you use to describe ...?
- a person
- the weather
- a meal
- a car
- a door or window
- the ground
- clothes
- eyes

3 In pairs, use the collocations to talk about recent experiences.

English in use
Describing extreme feelings and experiences

💬 It was unbelievable. I've never been so embarrassed in my life.

1 Decide which phrases in **A** could go before the expressions in **B**.

A		
I was absolutely ...	It was absolutely ...	It was ...
stunned.	hilarious.	an absolute nightmare.
petrified.	awful.	so embarrassing.
livid.	bizarre.	sheer bliss.
devastated.	wonderful.	a total disaster.
speechless.	brilliant.	really weird.

B	
I felt like bursting into tears.	I nearly hit the roof.
It frightened the life out of me.	I went bright red.
I could have died with embarrassment.	I'll never live it down.
I couldn't believe my eyes / ears.	I was in stitches.
I was scared stiff.	I nearly burst out laughing.
I was over the moon.	I couldn't keep a straight face.

2 🔲3 In pairs listen to six extracts from anecdotes, and predict which expressions from **1** the speaker will use next.

3 🔲4 Listen and compare your ideas.

Speak out

1 In pairs, **A** look at *p.105*, and **B** at *p.108*. Prepare your anecdotes.

2 In **A** / **B** pairs, tell your anecdotes.

3 Note down the main points of a real holiday anecdote.

4 In groups of four, tell each other your anecdotes.

Pronunciation

1 🔲2 Listen to a recording of some of the expressions in **1**. Write down the word or words with the main stress.

2 In pairs, practise repeating them.

Remember
- Think about how to introduce and end the anecdote.
- Use a range of expressions to describe extreme feelings and experiences.
- Use some collocations to describe details.

A BIT OF A PROBLEM

In this lesson

- Focus on expressing yourself more politely in English.
- Read and listen to understand specific words and phrases.
- Study and practise tentative language and ways of explaining problems.
- Practise making and dealing with complaints.

Speak for yourself

1 Read the questionnaire. Tick (✓) the option which best describes you.

1 At a restaurant, your meal is not very hot. Do you ...?
- demand to see the manager.
- ask the waiter to heat it up for you.
- grumble to your companions, but avoid making a scene.
- eat it, but write to the manager later.

2 You bought a cassette recorder which turns out to be faulty. Do you ...?
- accept a credit note or exchange.
- ask firmly for your money back.
- go to the shop and demand to see the manager.
- shrug your shoulders and forget about it.

3 The flight you reserved a seat on turns out to be overbooked. Do you ...?
- wait patiently to be put on another flight.
- shout at the check-in assistant.
- insist that you are given a seat on the plane.
- complain vociferously to your fellow passengers.

4 You called the plumber but he never turned up. Do you ...?
- not make a fuss but say you'll take your custom elsewhere in future.
- threaten to tell the whole neighbourhood how unreliable he is.
- phone and ask him to come immediately.
- forget about it.

2 In pairs, compare your ideas. When did you last make a complaint? What happened?

Reading
Finding specific information

1 Read the extracts about how to complain. What advice is given for each situation?

2 Would the same advice apply in your country?

3 ⏱ **Against the clock!** In pairs, you have eight minutes to decide on the meaning of the words and expressions in **bold**.

know your rights

AT A RESTAURANT

When you eat out, whether in a café, restaurant, or pub, you enter into a contract with those providing the service. Under the contract, the standard of service and food provided must be reasonable. What is reasonable will depend on many factors, such as the type of establishment and the price paid. Should the food or service **fail to live up to your expectations**, it is best to act immediately, when there is the maximum opportunity of **rectifying the situation**. Your complaint should first be addressed to the waiter serving you. Only when the waiter is unable or unwilling to put things right should you complain to the manager. If you have failed through reasonable discussion to put things right satisfactorily, you could consider making a deduction from your bill.

FAULTY GOODS

Before you return a faulty item, be clear exactly what it is that you want. Do you want a repair, replacement, or full refund, or will you accept a credit note? It is always a good idea to ask to see the manager or person in authority, to show that **you mean business** right from the start. It is important to adopt the right tone. The last thing you want to do is **antagonize** the person you are dealing with. Make your complaint politely but firmly, and avoid **getting into a row**. Wherever possible, take your receipt or other proof of purchase. Find out what your legal rights are; this will give you confidence, and put you in a stronger bargaining position.

OVERBOOKING OF FLIGHTS

Some airlines deliberately overfill their flights on the assumption that several **would-be passengers** will cancel, leaving a neat fully-booked flight. Should you be unable to get a seat on the flight you booked, **the airline is in breach of contract**, and may have to pay you compensation for whatever loss you have suffered, provided it is one that could not reasonably have been foreseen.

BROKEN APPOINTMENTS

If a repair man has **undertaken** to call at a certain time, and either doesn't turn up, or arrives very late, he has broken part of his contract, and **you are entitled to compensation**. Deduct a reasonable sum from the bill for wasted time and inconvenience, and send a letter explaining why you have paid less than asked. You can claim for extra telephone calls, and additional expenses such as using a launderette for your washing, if it is your washing machine that needs repairing. If you have had to take time off work, **you can claim for loss of earnings** too.

Which? Publications

Did you notice...?

💬 **Should** the food or service fail to live up to your expectations, it is best to act immediately.

💬 **Should** you be unable to get a seat on the flight you booked, the airline may have to pay you compensation.

1 How could you express the first part of these sentences in another way?

2 How does the use of *should* alter the style of the sentences?

Listening
Focus on politeness

1 In pairs, improvise these conversations.
- A customer phones a mail order company to complain that a book has not arrived.
- A software retailer phones a wholesale outlet to complain that he hasn't received the number of CD-ROMs he ordered.

2 🔲 Listen and compare your conversations with those on the tape.

3 Turn to the Tapescript on *p.117* and listen again. Highlight any words / expressions that make the conversations more polite.

4 Did you use any of the polite expressions in your conversations?

1 🔊 2 Listen to some negative sentences. Note down the stressed words in each.

2 Notice how the words are linked. How is the final /t/ pronounced before a consonant?

3 Listen again and repeat.

Vocabulary
Explaining problems

1 ☀ **Against the clock!** You have three minutes to read the complaints and decide if they could refer to ...

- a car
- central heating
- a computer
- a toilet
- a TV set
- a camera

1 The screen keeps going blank.
2 I'm having problems downloading things.
3 I can't get it to go into second gear.
4 It won't flush properly.
5 It keeps crashing.

6 I've been having problems with the thermostat.
7 The shutter keeps jamming.
8 I can't get it to start.
9 It won't come on.
10 It keeps stalling.

2 Which of these problems have you experienced?

3 Note down possible problems with different appliances.

4 In pairs, ask and answer about your problems, using some of the language in **1**. Give advice.

It keeps ...   It won't ...   I can't get it to ...   I'm having problems ...

Language work
Tentative language

> **Polite expressions**
>
> It is common in English to use tentative language if there is a disagreement or misunderstanding, to prevent the other person 'losing face'.
>
> **Perhaps / Maybe** ... there's been a mistake.
> **Are you sure** you ordered a hundred?
> **I feel certain / I'm pretty sure** ... we ordered two boxes.
> **I understood / I thought** I would be seen to today.

1 Make these statements more polite using one of the expressions above.

1 Did you turn the machine on?
2 I posted the letter last week.
3 You said I could exchange it if it was the wrong size.
4 We never promised to have it ready by Thursday.
5 You promised I could have a refund.
6 You told me you wanted ten copies, not twenty.
7 You don't know how to operate the machine.
8 You obviously didn't follow the instructions correctly.

I feel certain I ordered a steak...

💬 You **don't seem** to have sent us enough.

Even if you are sure there is a problem, use *seem* to sound more polite.

There seems **to be** a problem with the order.
It doesn't seem **to be printing** properly.
We seem **to have got lost**.

2 Focus on form Which three patterns follow the word *seem* above?

3 `○3` Listen to ten statements and make them sound more polite by using the correct form of *seem*.

4 In pairs, act out conversations using some of the problems in **3**.

English in use
Dealing with problems

🕐 **Against the clock!** You have three minutes to match expressions **1** to **12** to the headings.

Apologizing   Making a request   Expressing sympathy   Offering to help

1 I'm sorry about that.
2 I'll do my best to sort it out for you.
3 If you could just bear with me a couple of moments.
4 Sorry about the misunderstanding.
5 I don't suppose there's any way you could get it to me by tomorrow?
6 I'm sorry you've been inconvenienced.
7 I can understand why you're upset.
8 I'll get back to you as soon as I can.
9 I was rather hoping you could give me a refund.
10 I do understand.
11 I'll look into it.
12 I do apologize.

Speak out

1 In pairs, **A** and **B**, take it in turns to make a phone call to make and deal with complaints. **A** turn to *p.105* and **B** to *p.108*.

I'm phoning to …   I'm phoning about …

2 After the roleplays, decide …
- how successful the outcomes of the conversations were.
- how you would have dealt with these situations in your own country.

Remember

- Use a range of polite expressions.
- Use different expressions and language to explain problems.
- Concentrate on your intonation and word linking.

Follow-up

1 Think about a real problem you have had with something you have bought or ordered. Write a dialogue in which you complain.

2 If you are living in an English-speaking environment, note down examples of polite language you hear this week.

3 Choose three personal or household appliances, and think about things that can go wrong with them. Use your dictionary to research vocabulary to describe the problems.

21
TALKING PICTURES

In this lesson

- Discuss and describe films.
- Listen to people giving opinions.
- Focus on adjectives and expressions describing films.
- Study and practise adverb modifiers.
- Read quickly to understand the gist.

Speak for yourself

1 Look at the stills below and identify the films.

2 Which of the films is ...?

- a road movie
- a costume drama
- a psychological thriller
- a blockbuster
- a slapstick comedy
- a romantic comedy

3 What other film genres can you think of?

4 **What do you think?** Discuss these questions in groups of three.
   1 What types of film do you particularly like or dislike, and why?
   2 In general, do you prefer seeing films at the cinema or on video? Why?

Listening
Understanding opinions

1 **○1** Listen to a radio arts programme in which two people discuss *The Talented Mr Ripley*.
   1 What kind of film is it?
   2 Did they both like it?

2 Listen again and note down what they think of ...
   1 the film overall
   2 the acting
   3 the story
   4 the supporting actors
   5 the ending

3 **○2** Listen to two friends, Rob and Conal, discussing *The English Patient*. Did they both like it?

4 Listen again and say whether the statements are true or false.
   1 Conal thought the film was better than the book.
   2 Conal thought it was true to life.
   3 They both agreed it was a moving film.
   4 They were both impressed by the cinematography.

5 Write down five questions you could ask someone about a film.

6 **○3** Listen to someone asking about the film *Gladiator*. Did she ask the same questions?

7 Turn to the Tapescript on *p.118*, listen again, and note down what the speaker liked about the film.

Vocabulary
Expressions connected with films

1 In pairs, use the context to work out the meaning of these expressions.

　1 The director was unknown and couldn't get funding, so the film was **made on a shoe-string budget** with a **cast** of amateurs.

　2 It was a **box office smash** in America, and made millions of dollars, but in this country it was a **flop**.

　3 I planned to see the film after reading all the **rave reviews** in the papers, but seeing the **trailer** at the cinema put me off going.

　4 It's a faithful **adaptation** of the Dickens novel.

　5 Patrick never leaves the cinema till all the **credits** have been shown.

　6 It has become a **cult film** for a certain group of **cinema-goers**, but it doesn't appeal to a **mass audience**.

　7 It **tells the tale of** a family of immigrant workers and is a bleak **portrayal of** life in turn-of-the-century New York.

　8 The **opening sequence** starts with a **close-up** of the heroine on the train.

　9 The **screenplay** is by Tom Stoppard, and John Williams composed the **score**.

　10 My brother is a real **film buff**; he can list all the films any director has made.

Adjectives to describe films

2 ☀ **Against the clock!** In two groups, **A** and **B**, you have five minutes to check the meaning of the adjectives in your box.

3 Which adjectives suggest a negative opinion?

A			
action-packed	depressing	pacey	slow-moving
moving	poignant	predictable	powerful
impressive	entertaining	enjoyable	charming
well-received	offbeat	unconventional	epic
subtle	understated	compelling	overstated

B			
hilarious	flat	dramatic	amusing
oversimplified	sentimental	soppy	over-romantic
perceptive	gripping	insightful	thought-provoking
corny	brilliant	bleak	dated
overrated	underrated	stylish	intelligent

4 In **A** / **B** pairs, test your partner. Choose some words from your box and ask for a definition.

5 Which adjectives describe the kind of films you like / dislike?

6 Complete the rule.

In compound adjectives, the stress usually falls on the _____ word.

When the first word is a noun, the stress usually falls on the _____ word.

7 🔊5 Mark the stress on these words. Listen and check.

1 good-looking	5 bullet-proof	9 part-time
2 late-night	6 first-class	10 low-paid
3 old-fashioned	7 suntanned	11 mass-produced
4 air-conditioned	8 off-peak	12 candlelit

Language work
Adverb modifiers

It is very common to use adjectives with adverb modifiers.

It was **really** gripping.
The acting was **pretty** poor.
I'd heard it was **a bit** over-romantic.
The ending was **rather** inconclusive.
I thought it was **quite** moving.

1 Look at the above examples.
   1 Which of the adverbs are mainly used in spoken, informal English?
   2 Which one is not normally used with adjectives with a positive meaning?

2 Look again at the adjectives on *p.71*. Use some of them with adverb modifiers to talk about films you have seen.

English in use
Talking about films

1 Read and complete the following ways of talking about films.

Pronunciation

1 ⟨06⟩ Listen and write down the ten sentences.

2 Listen again and repeat, paying attention to the /ɪ/ sound.

3 In pairs, practise saying the sentences.

Describing films

What _____ of film is it?	It's a kind of romantic comedy.
What's it _____?	It's basically about his fall from grace.
Who's _____ it?	Matt Damon plays the lead.
Who's it _____ by?	Woody Allen.
Did it have a happy _____?	No, I was in tears at the end.

It's _____ in America in the 1950s.
It was _____ in New Zealand.
It's _____ on a novel by Graham Greene.
It's _____ seven Oscar nominations.

Discussing films

Have you seen any good films _____?
What did you think _____ it? / Is it _____ good ? / Is it _____ seeing?
What did you _____ _____ the camera work / the special effects?

It _____ up to / didn't _____ up to my expectations.
I _____ the score / cinematography.
I liked the _____ where he carries her draped in a sheet ...

Describing the plot

Focus on form Which verb form is used to recount events?

He starts off as a general ... he becomes a gladiator and has to fight for his life ... he ends up being killed.

Complete the sentence with the correct prepositions.

_____ the beginning she doesn't like him but halfway _____ the film he saves her dog's life, and _____ the end they get married.

2 Think of a film that you have seen. Make notes about the theme, the setting, the plot, and the main actors.

3 In groups of three, describe your film to other people. They guess which film it is. Don't make it too easy!

Reading
Speed reading

1 🕐 **Against the clock!** In two groups, **A** and **B**, you have five minutes to read about films showing at the Phoenix cinema. **A** turn to *p.106* and **B** to *p.109*.

   1 Decide what kind of film each one is.

   2 Underline words that describe the films.

2 Decide which film appeals to you most, and why.

3 In **A / B** pairs, decide on a film that you would like to see together.

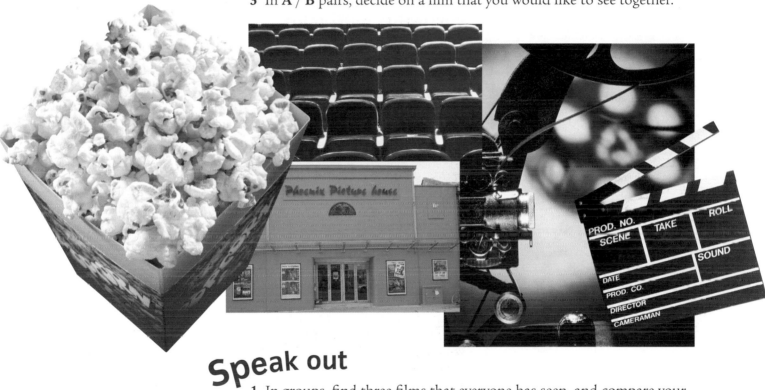

Speak out

1 In groups, find three films that everyone has seen, and compare your opinions.

2 Ask other people about a film they have seen recently that you have not seen. Decide whether you would like to go and see it.

Remember
- Use a range of vocabulary and expressions to describe films.
- Use different adjectives and adverb modifiers.
- Use the present simple to describe the plot of a film.

Follow-up
1 Watch a film with a friend and discuss it afterwards in English.
2 Read film reviews in a film magazine or on the Internet. Add useful words and phrases to your vocabulary book.
3 Prepare to give a review in class of a favourite film, saying why you like it.
4 Write a paragraph about a film you have seen, but without mentioning the title. Pass it to a friend for correction. In the next lesson, put the reviews on the wall and try to identify as many of the films as possible.

22 WHAT HAVE YOU BEEN UP TO?

In this lesson

- Listen for exact words.
- Focus on verb forms to talk about recent activities and actions.
- Look at uses of vague language.

Did you notice...?

💬 I've **been** to Edinburgh.

💬 I've **been** on a couple of trips.

💬 I've **been** a bit busy with work.

Does *been* act as the past participle of *be* or *go* in these examples?

Speak for yourself

1 Note down four things you would talk about with a friend you haven't seen recently.

2 In pairs, improvise a conversation.

Listening

Following short conversations

1 📀1 Listen to two conversations. Note down recent activities.

2 How well do the people know each other? How do you know?

3 Listen again, and complete the sentences.

1 Adam, hello, how are you, I _____ .
2 Yeah, I suppose you _____ .
3 Mm, very busy at work but mostly _____ .
4 Right. Ah, you've always been keen on travelling, so _____ ?
5 Very cold and rainy, but still very pleasant, and _____ .
6 And how about yourself, what _____ ?

1 Well, um, I _____ .
2 I've been a bit busy with work. I _____ .
3 Oh, where _____ ?

English in use

Recent actions and activities

1 Turn to the Tapescript on *p.118*. Which verb forms were used most?

2 **Focus on form** Complete the rules.

Use _____ to talk about regular recent activities.

Use _____ to announce a single recent action.

Use _____ to give further details about a recent action.

3 Did you use the same verb forms in *Speak for yourself*?

4 Look at these examples.

I've done a bit of travelling.   I've been studying quite a lot.

I've been doing a lot of overtime.   I haven't been studying very much.

Can you use *a bit of / a lot of, a lot,* and *very much*...

- with positive / negative verb forms?
- to qualify nouns or verbs?

1 **○2** Listen and write down six sentences.

2 Listen again and mark the word, or words, with the main stress.

3 How are *been* and *have* pronounced?

4 In pairs, practise saying the sentences.

5 **⚘ Against the clock!** You have four minutes to write down two examples of recent activities / actions for each of the statements.

⤷ I'm really stressed. ⤷ I've put on weight.
⤷ I'm very fit. ⤷ My social life is great!

Vocabulary
Vague language

It is very common in spoken English to use vague expressions ...
- when it is not important to give exact details.
- when you are not sure of the exact details.

1 Why do you think the expressions in **bold** were used in the conversations in *Listening*?

  1 I've been doing **various bits and pieces** – bits of this and bits of that.

  2 I met **a few** people, and went out for meals, and didn't get enough sleep, **and that kind of thing**.

  3 I've been on **a couple of** trips.

  4 I've been organizing candles and cakes and presents **and so on**.

2 **○3** Listen to four conversations. Note down examples of vague language.

3 Listen again with the Tapescript on *p.118* and check your ideas.

4 Match the expressions you heard in **2** to one of these headings.

  Approximation   Generalization   Word substitution

5 **○4** Listen and answer the questions using vague expressions.

Speak out

Remember
- Use appropriate verb forms to describe recent activities and actions.
- Use vague expressions where appropriate.
- Concentrate on correct sentence stress.

In groups of three, **A**, **B**, and **C**, toss a coin to play the game. **A** talk about recent activities, **B** ask questions, and **C** monitor. Swap roles.

1 food and drink START ☞	2 concerts and plays	3 family and friends	4 study	5 travel
12 cars		1 square HEADS / TAILS 2 squares		6 work
11 housework	10 letters	9 sports	8 TV	7 books

23 FUTURE DEVELOPMENTS

In this lesson

- Read for gist and detailed understanding.
- Study and practise using multi-word expressions.
- Focus on making predictions and using future time expressions.
- Practise making a presentation.

Did you notice…?

💬 *Nowhere is the effect of this seen more clearly than on the Internet.*

In formal English, the verb is inverted after some sentence beginnings. This emphasizes the main point of the sentence.

Speak for yourself

1 In which professional fields is English the major language for global communication?

2 In pairs, decide whether you think these statements are true or false.
1 English will be less important in the future than it is now.
2 The US will continue to be the most important economic power.
3 The Internet is developing its own variety of English.
4 Most users of English will speak American English.
5 In a few years, there will be more people speaking English as a second language than English as a first language.

Reading
Reading for gist and detail

1 🕐 **Against the clock!** You have five minutes to read the whole text and match each paragraph to one of the headings.

New varieties of English   Ownership of the English language
The future of English   A period of transition
English in the world today

2 Look again at the statements in *Speak for yourself* and decide whether the author considers them to be true or false.

3 **What do you think?** In pairs, answer the questions.
1 Which predictions in the text do you find the most surprising?
2 Have you noticed any examples of 'net English' or other specialist uses?

4 Which of these sentence beginnings are followed by inversions?
Rarely…   Everywhere…   Never…   Only in America…
Sometimes…   Only when…   Hardly…   Under no circumstances…

The Future of English

A

At first sight, there seems little likelihood that the global popularity of English will diminish. After all, it is the first language of capitalism, of international commerce and trade, and of the Internet. It has more cultural resources, in the sense of works of literature, films, and television programmes, than any other language. It is the main language of newspapers, airports and air traffic control, international business and academic conferences, science and technology, diplomacy, sport, international competitions, pop music, and advertising. But the future of English may well not be straightforward, and there are reasons why we ought to take stock and reassess its place in the world.

B

There is a general awareness of change at the start of a new century, but no clear vision of where it may all be leading. The economic dominance of countries such as Britain and the USA, which helped circulate English in the new market economies of the world, is being eroded by the growth of Asian economies. The populations of the rich countries are ageing, and in the coming decades young adults with disposable incomes will be found in Asia and Latin America, rather than the US and Europe. The start of the twenty-first century is likely to be a period of global transition, with a new order emerging. It can be expected to be an uncomfortable and at times traumatic experience for many of the world's citizens.

C

As the world is in transition, so the English language is itself taking new forms. In many parts of the world, as English is taken into the fabric of social life, it develops a momentum and vitality of its own, diverging increasingly from the kind of English spoken in Britain or North America. English is also used for more purposes than ever before. Everywhere it is at the leading edge of technological and scientific development, new thinking in economics and management, new literature and entertainment genres. These give rise to new vocabularies, grammatical forms, and ways of speaking and writing. Nowhere is the effect of this expansion of English into new domains seen more clearly than in communication on the Internet and the development of 'net English'.

D

But the language is, in another way, at a critical moment in its global career; within a decade or so, the number of people who speak English as a second language will exceed the number of native speakers. The implications of this are likely to be far-reaching. The centre of authority regarding the language will shift from native speakers; their literature and television may no longer provide the focal point of a global English language culture, their teachers no longer form the unchallenged authoritative models for students.

E

It seems, then, that the future for English may well be a complex and plural one. The language will grow in usage and variety, yet simultaneously diminish in global importance. It may cease to be the most important language, sharing that role instead with other languages such as Spanish and Chinese. In short, the future of English will be more complex, more demanding of understanding and more challenging for the position of native-speaking countries than has hitherto been supposed.

'The Future of English' by David Graddol

I can't quite get the hang of this!

Vocabulary
Multi-word expressions

💬 There are reasons why we ought to **take stock**.

💬 These **give rise to** new vocabularies.

A	B
keep track of	make fun of
take issue with	take advantage of
give rise to	get the hang of
take charge of	make the best of
come to terms with	take stock of

1 Decide whether to choose the noun or the verb part of expressions like these to look up in a dictionary.

2 In two groups, **A** and **B**, check the meaning of the expressions and note down an example sentence for each.

3 In **A** / **B** pairs, read your sentences to your partner without the expressions. They complete the sentences.

English in use
Predictions with *will*

1 In pairs, match descriptions **a** to **e** to the expressions in **bold**.

  a it will definitely happen   **d** it probably won't happen

  b it will probably happen   **e** it definitely won't happen

  c it may happen

  1 **I'm certain that** English will die out.

  2 **I doubt whether** they'll find a cure for AIDS.

  3 **I would imagine that** world supplies of oil will run out.

  4 **There's no doubt that** we'll discover life on another planet.

  5 **It's highly unlikely that** the whale will become extinct.

  6 **There's a chance that** scientists will be able to reverse global warming.

  7 **There's no way that** America will elect a black president.

  8 **The chances are that** solar power will be the most common form of energy.

2 **What do you think?** Do you agree with the statements? Express your opinion by using a different expression where necessary.

Pronunciation
1 🔊 **1** Listen and notice the pronunciation of *will*.
2 Listen again and repeat.

Predictions with the infinitive

💬 There's **unlikely to be** a drop in interest rates.

💬 It's **likely to rain** tomorrow.

💬 Air fares **are bound to go up** in price.

💬 House prices **are bound not to keep** rising at this rate.

3 **Focus on form** Complete the rule.

Use: subject + _____ + _____ + _____

4 Look at the text on *p.77* again and underline all the phrases with *will*, the infinitive, or other forms of future reference.

May and *might* can be used to make predictions. They can be more or less sure according to which word is stressed.

1 🔊2 Listen to six pairs of sentences and say which word is stressed.

2 Which prediction in each pair is more certain?

5 Use a form of *bound (not) to* or *likely / unlikely to* to expand the prompts into sentences.

1 It / be hot next week
2 Computers / get cheaper
3 Brazil / win the next World Cup
4 Jeans / go out of fashion
5 We / have a test next week
6 There / be a party at the end of the course

Language work
Future time expressions

by the middle of this century	in the next few years
in five years' time	within a decade or so
(not) in the foreseeable future	(not) in my lifetime
in the near future	in the coming decade
one day	in the distant future

1 Use one of the time expressions to say when these predictions might come true.

1 Electrical appliances will be operated by voice control.
2 There will be a world court of human rights.
3 Traditional surgery will be replaced by gene therapy.
4 Malaria will have been eradicated.
5 People will be wearing computers on their wrists.
6 We will have obliterated half the world's species.
7 Trips to the moon will be commonplace.
8 People will be driving zero emission cars.
9 Everyone in the world will be speaking English.
10 There will be a world currency.

2 Rephrase each prediction with an expression from *English in use*. In pairs, compare your ideas.

Speak out

1 In groups of three, decide what future developments there will be in the next ten years in three of these areas.

- holidays
- in the home
- fashion
- entertainment
- language learning
- transport
- shopping
- in the workplace

2 Design a service or a product to meet future market needs in one area.

3 Give a presentation to the class, outlining your predictions of future trends and how your product will meet future market needs.

- Use a range of expressions to predict the future.
- Use future time expressions to say when things may happen.
- Use different multi-word expressions from the lesson.
- Concentrate on sentence stress when using *may* and *might*.

1 Write predictions about political, sporting, or cultural events in your country, or about class members.

2 Discuss the news with an English-speaking friend, making predictions about what might happen in the next few days.

3 Research facts and figures on the global use of English in reference books or on the Internet. Write a list or make a poster displaying what you have found out.

4 Find examples of 'net' English and other areas where the language is changing or used in different forms.

Speak for yourself

1 Why do people climb mountains? Does it appeal to you?

2 If you were going to go on a mountaineering expedition ...
- what would you have to do before the trip?
- what could go wrong on the trip?

3 Look at the photos. What might have happened before or after?

Listening
Taking notes

1 🔊1 In two groups, **A** and **B**, **A** listen to Michael. Make notes on ...
- how the trip was planned.
- the peak they chose to climb.
- how successful the climb was.
- the weather.
- four regrets he has.

🔊2 **B** listen to Julie. Make notes on ...
- why she is on crutches.
- the temperature at night.
- her experience on the summit.
- a problem coming downhill.
- two things she did wrong.

2 In **A / B** pairs, use your notes to retell the stories.

Mount Everest

Mount Kenya

3 Listen to both stories and complete these extracts.

1 With hindsight, would you have done anything differently?
Well, _____ .

2 On the whole, the whole trip was a great success, and _____ , but _____ in the day-to-day running of things, and not been portered and guided all the way because it did leave me with a lot of spare time, and a lot of cold weather and long dark nights

_____ .

3 With a bit more time, _____ , and perhaps found a more interesting way, but I think on the whole, considering it was our first trip, we _____ .

4 Doing all that running down the mountain caused pain in my knees and
_____ and remembered the

advice that was given, and _____
is seek medical help sooner really because I had a pain the next day.

5 Oh no, but you're glad you did it? Well, _____ .

Language work
Past conditionals

1 Focus on form Look at these sentences and complete the rules.

1 If she'd been looking where she was going, she wouldn't have fallen.
2 If we'd consulted the map, we might not have got lost.
3 We could have reached the summit if we'd set off earlier.
4 If she hadn't climbed the mountain so fast, she wouldn't have a bad knee and wouldn't be walking on crutches today.

To imagine different past consequences of a past event use ...
If + _____ in the conditional clause, and _____ in the result clause.

To imagine different present consequences of a past event use ...
If + _____ in the conditional clause, and _____ in the result clause.

2 [○3] Listen to ten statements, and make sentences starting with *If* ... .
My friend suggested the idea, and so I went to the Himalayas.
If my friend hadn't suggested the idea, I wouldn't have gone to the Himalayas.

English in use
Expressing regret and lack of regret

1 In pairs, highlight the expressions which express regret.

1 In retrospect, I wish I'd chosen my companions more carefully.
2 It's just as well I started taking malaria pills before I went.
3 With hindsight, we should have checked the forecast before setting off.
4 Luckily, we were able to book a sleeping compartment.
5 Thank goodness we took a first aid kit with us.
6 I have no regrets about the route we took.
7 Looking back, I'm glad we took out insurance before the trip.
8 As it turned out, we needn't have taken our waterproofs.
9 I wish I'd gone for longer.
10 If only I hadn't tried to stroke that elephant!
11 I'd have liked to visit the islands as well.
12 It's a pity we didn't get the chance to go on a guided tour.

2 Focus on form In pairs, look at exercise 1 again and answer **1** to **3**.

1 Which verb form is used after *I wish* and *If only* to express past regret?
2 Why do we say *we were able to book*, and not *we could book*?
3 Which two modal verbs are used and which form is used after them?

3 ⏱ **Against the clock!** In pairs, you have three minutes to choose a headline and make five sentences to express regret and lack of regret people might feel about the situation.

Vocabulary
Discourse markers

🗩 On the whole, the trip was a great success.
🗩 In the end, there was an odd collection of people.

1 ⏱ **Against the clock!** In pairs, you have three minutes to choose a discourse marker to continue each sentence.

in practice	deep down	in retrospect	in the end
in public	in the current situation	in reality	on the other
in the flesh	in the long term		

1 At first I didn't really take to him, but …
2 In theory the plan looks feasible, but …
3 At the time it seemed like a good idea, but …
4 In private he has a great sense of humour, but …
5 On paper she has the right qualifications, but …
6 On the surface she seems rather stand-offish, but …
7 On screen she looks stunning, but …
8 Under normal circumstances I'd be happy to join the expedition, but …
9 In the short term we'd make a profit, but …
10 On the one hand I'd really like to go to the party, but …

2 Complete each sentence in an appropriate way.

Pronunciation

1 🔊4 Listen to eight sentences and notice the pronunciation of *have*.
2 Listen again and repeat.

Holidaymakers stranded for two days in airport as airline goes bust

MILLIONS LOST AS STOCK MARKET CRASHES

Couple survive three weeks at sea in inflatable life raft

Pronunciation

1 🔊5 Listen to the sentences in *Against the clock!* Notice the stress and intonation patterns.
2 Listen again and repeat.
3 Read your complete sentences to another pair, paying attention to correct stress and intonation.

Mountain idioms

1 In pairs, use the context to explain the expressions in **bold**.

1 The team **reached their peak** at the end of last season, but from then on they seem to have **gone downhill**.

2 Some people think you're **over the hill** when you reach sixty, but I feel **at the peak** of my mental powers.

3 She gave up writing **at the height of** her career to have a family.

4 I know his behaviour wasn't very good, but I still think it was a bit **over the top** to exclude him from school.

5 It will be **an uphill struggle** to survive against foreign competition.

6 The world won't come to an end just because you've failed your driving test; stop **making a mountain out of a molehill**.

7 We've **had our ups and downs** over the years, but we're still friends.

8 I've been **searching high and low** for my keys; they've disappeared.

2 Check the expressions in a dictionary. Use five expressions to write true sentences.

Speak out

1 Choose two situations which you have experienced. Make notes on how you are going to describe the event and express your feelings.

- an expedition • a journey • a holiday   • a performance • an interview
- a course   • a party   • a celebration • a speech   • an exam

Remember

- Ask and answer questions using past conditional forms.
- Use a range of expressions to talk about regret and lack of regret.
- Use a range of discourse markers and idioms.
- Concentrate on using the contracted form of *have* and correct intonation.

2 In groups of three, describe your event. Ask and answer questions.

- What would you have done if ...?
- Could you have ...?
- Do you regret ...?
- Do you have any regrets about ...?
- Are you glad you ...?

Follow-up

1 Write a paragraph about one of the events in *Speak out*.

2 Ask people you know if they have any regrets about events in their lives.

3 Look up the following expressions in a monolingual dictionary, and add them to your vocabulary book.

in the event	as a last resort	for that matter	from the word go
in due course	on the off chance	on the contrary	on reflection
to no avail	having said that	all being well	as it happens

4 Practise saying conditional sentences aloud with the correct pronunciation.

PRACTICE

01

1 Adjectives

Complete the conversations in two different ways. Use a synonym and an opposite adjective.

1 Isn't it freezing!
   a Yes, it's really _____ , isn't it?
   b Yes, it isn't very _____ , is it?

2 This room is absolutely filthy!
   a Yes, it's very _____ .
   b Yes, it's not very _____ , is it?

3 I thought the film was really tedious.
   a Yes, it was rather _____ , wasn't it?
   b Yes, it wasn't very _____ , was it?

4 What an idiotic thing to say!
   a Yes, it was rather _____ , wasn't it?
   b Yes, it wasn't very _____ , was it?

5 Jon said the food was disgusting.
   a He was right! It was really _____ .
   b Yes, it wasn't very _____ .

2 Conversational exchanges

Choose the most appropriate response and explain your choice.

1 Allow me to introduce Jeremy Broad.
   a How are you?
   b How do you do?

2 Do you mind if I smoke?
   a Yes, I mind.
   b I'd rather you didn't, actually.

3 Well, I'd better be off.
   a Nice to meet you.
   b Nice meeting you.

4 Do you come here often?
   a Yes, I do.
   b Every weekend. And you?

5 Wonderful food!
   a Yes, fantastic.
   b Yes, I think so.

6 Have you got the time, by any chance?
   a I make it ten thirty.
   b The time for what?

02

1 Expressions connected with time

Rewrite the sentences using the KEY word. Check on *p.07*.

1 I had to get up very early in the morning.   CRACK
2 Production at the factory has been temporarily suspended.   TIME
3 Dinner will be served at 8.30 precisely.   DOT
4 We made a sudden decision to have a party.   SPUR
5 You really should look for a job immediately.   TIME
6 The ambulance arrived just before it was too late.   TIME
7 It's ages since I went to a circus.   DONKEY'S
8 There used to be a staff canteen, but that was before I started here. TIME

2 Multi-word verbs

Complete the sentences with the correct words. Check on *p.08*.

1 I love lingering ____ breakfast when I'm on holiday.
2 It's hard to keep ____ ____ all the changes in computer technology.
3 One of these days I'll get ____ ____ reading *War and Peace*.
4 I keep putting ____ cleaning the car.
5 It looks as if the rain is easing ____ now.
6 Unless you do the washing up every day, it tends to pile ____ .
7 At weekends I enjoy pottering ____ in the garden.
8 I missed two weeks of school so now I have a lot of catching ____ to do.

3 Describing trends and changes

Correct the mistake in each sentence.

1 The price of home computers has **reduced** dramatically.
2 More and more people **buy** air tickets on line nowadays.
3 In the past six months, the rate of inflation **doubled**.
4 I **am having** less and less free time these days.
5 There has been a steady increase **of** the number of car thefts.
6 It's getting **more and more easy** to find a job.
7 The divorce rate has increased **strongly** over the last ten years.
8 These days, people are working **increasingly longer** hours.

03

1 Adjectives to describe food

Find fourteen words to describe food, going from top to bottom, left to right, and diagonally.

```
B A F G Y M B O P D C L
H L L B A T E N D E R I
I O A E D A F F C K C G
E V W N A S T J E F U H
K E P V D T E D U B S T
G R E A S Y N A M I I L
U C B D E O B J O T C F
B O V E R R I P E O K Y
T O N A M L J L H U L A
R K F R E S H A E G Y C
E E D S A I R I C H H B
S D O C P W A N O D A G
```

2 Food idioms

Complete the sentences using a food idiom. Check on *p.12*.

1 I don't know how he can afford to run two cars. He gets …
2 You can go for a picnic if you like, but I'm afraid picnics aren't my …
3 He should work out exactly what needs doing instead of coming up with …
4 My nephew will enjoy the chocolate biscuits and ice-cream. He's got …
5 I'd love to come out with you this evening but I'm afraid I've got …
6 Sally wants me to buy her a new dress so she keeps trying to …
7 Why don't you look for a job? I'm tired of being the only …
8 Thank you for that stimulating speech. I'm sure it's given everyone …

3 Frequency adverbs and adverbial phrases

Use a frequency adverb or adverbial phrase to describe your own habits.

1 I eat fast food.
   I hardly ever eat fast food / I don't often eat fast food / I eat fast food every other day.
2 I try out new recipes.
3 I say grace before a meal.
4 I have a cigarette after my meal.
5 I have breakfast in bed.
6 I eat ready-made meals.
7 I eat my main meal after 9.00 in the evening.
8 I eat watching TV.
9 I have friends round for a barbecue.
10 I have wine with my main meal.
11 I prepare a packed lunch.
12 I order a takeaway.

04

1 Work and study collocations

Match the words below with the appropriate verb.

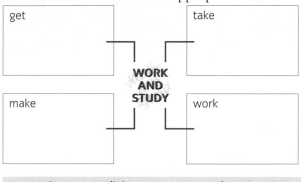

promotion	a living	early retirement
a profit	progress	part-time
a grant	the sack	a career change
an exam	maternity leave	in shifts
good grades	a gap year	a fortune
full-time	flexi-time	a rise

2 Revision of verb forms

Complete the text with a correct form of the verb in brackets.

7th April 2001

Dear Sir / Madam,

I am writing to apply for the position of Adoptions Co-ordinator, as advertised in yesterday's edition of *The Guardian*.

As you will see from the enclosed CV, I [1] _____ (study) Sociology and Psychology at Nottingham University, where I [2] _____ (obtain) an upper second class degree. I [3] _____ (work) in the field of social work ever since I [4] _____ (graduate) in 1996. From 1996 to 1999, I [5] _____ (be) employed by Nottingham Social Services as a social worker. Since then, I [6] _____ (have) extensive experience of adoption work. Over the past four years I [7] _____ (specialize) in adoptions and foster care, and [8] _____ (lead) workshops on adoption procedures for teams within the Nottingham area. I [9] _____ (currently / work) for Derbyshire Social Services Department, where my duties [10] _____ (include) co-ordinating adoption teams within the Derbyshire area. I [11] _____ (also / study) part-time for a Master's degree in Social Work.

I [12] _____ (feel) the post you [13] _____ (offer) will allow me to develop my expertise in team management, and that I [14] _____ (possess) the necessary skills and experience to do the job successfully.

I look forward to hearing from you.

Yours sincerely,

Alyson Matthews

Alyson Matthews

05

1 Relationships vocabulary

Decide whether these sentences are logical (L) or illogical (I).

1 He had a crush on her so he tried to chat her up.
2 I went off Tim because we're on the same wavelength.
3 Sarah is having a fling with her other half.
4 Paul and Clare really hit it off so they decided to split up.
5 She's still got a soft spot for him, so she wants to make it up.
6 They fell out because they didn't see eye to eye on anything.
7 I used to think the world of him, but now he's grown on me.
8 Even though he's a terrible flirt, he's never been unfaithful to his wife.
9 They went on a blind date, and it was love at first sight.
10 We share a house, but we're not actually living together.

2 Paying compliments

Match compliments **1** to **10** with answers **a** to **j**.

1 I like your bracelet!
2 You're looking well.
3 What a sweet little puppy!
4 Didn't she play beautifully?
5 This trip was such a good idea.
6 What lovely handwriting you've got!
7 You dealt with that customer really well.
8 Doesn't your garden look gorgeous?
9 Great speech!
10 Your children are so well-behaved!

a Oh, it's terribly overgrown really.
b Yes, isn't he adorable!
c Thanks. I've just come back from holiday.
d Do you think so? I was really nervous.
e Yes, I thought it would do you good to get away.
f Thank you. I almost lost my cool with him, to be honest.
g They're little monsters, actually.
h Thanks. It was a present for my eighteenth birthday.
i Yes, I think it's the best recital I've heard her give.
j Thank you. Everyone says it's neat.

3 So, such, such a, really

Complete the sentences with *so*, *such*, *such a*, or *really*. Check on *p.19*.

1 I've put on _____ much weight that I can't get into my jeans.
2 He's _____ fussy about punctuality, so get there on time.
3 I've got _____ little time that I can't keep up with everything.
4 Katy always makes me laugh. She's _____ good company.
5 We had _____ nice time that we didn't want to come home.
6 Thanks for a lovely evening. We _____ enjoyed ourselves.
7 It was _____ bad weather that we decided to stay in.
8 I can't come out because I have a _____ heavy workload.
9 He was _____ fed up that he answered a lonely hearts ad.
10 She was under _____ pressure that she had a breakdown.

06

1 Two-part nouns

Rewrite the sentences using the KEY words. Check on *p.21*.

1 Are you expecting many people to attend the meeting?	TURNOUT
2 Let me know what happens as a result of the treatment.	OUTCOME
3 We are expecting that fewer people will be recruited this year.	CUTBACK
4 Violence broke out at last night's football cup final.	OUTBREAK
5 We have had problems with our attempt to launch the satellite.	SETBACK
6 Could you let me know about your recent research?	UPDATE
7 Talks between the management and unions have broken down.	BREAKDOWN
8 We will introduce tough new measures to combat hooliganism.	CRACKDOWN
9 How much business did you do last month?	TURNOVER
10 Scientists have discovered an important new way to treat heart disease.	BREAKTHROUGH

2 Articles

Complete the text with *a*, *an*, *the*, or no article.

1 _____ man in Essex has discovered 2 _____ painting by Picasso in 3 _____ rubbish dump near his house. 4 _____ painting was stolen from 5 _____ private collection in London six months ago and its owners had offered 6 _____ reward of £250,000 for 7 _____ information leading to 8 _____ discovery of 9 _____ masterpiece. 10 _____ man, who came across 11 _____ painting when out walking his dog near 12 _____ dump, has said he will spend 13 _____ money on 14 _____ yacht to travel around 15 _____ world. 16 _____ detectives are still investigating 17 _____ theft of five other paintings reported missing from 18 _____ collection during 19 _____ same robbery.

3 Reacting to news

Respond to each piece of news and add a question.

💬 1 My sister's having a baby.
   Is she? Fantastic! When's it due?
💬 2 I've just been burgled.
💬 3 Guess what! I've just won £500!
💬 4 The bus is late again.
💬 5 My mother's not very well.
💬 6 Hey, guess what! I've just been promoted.
💬 7 Apparently an elephant's escaped from the zoo.

07

1 Asking for information

Write the words in the correct order and add punctuation.

1 could me if you wonder I help
2 this idea to you do Paddington if any have train goes
3 price about to ringing of Malta enquire I'm to the flights
4 tube you where the sorry nearest know is station do
5 Sylvia's you happen do of you birth know date to don't
6 find me tell the excuse you can loo me I can where
7 know the suppose I where gone caretaker has don't you

2 Colloquial responses

Answer these questions about your teacher or a class member, using a colloquial expression.

1 When's his / her birthday?
2 How long has he / she been teaching?
3 How does he / she travel to work?
4 Has he / she got any children?
5 What kind of music does he / she like?
6 What does he / she do in his / her free time?
7 What's his / her favourite colour?
8 Has he / she got any pets?
9 What languages does he / she speak?
10 What does he / she do after the class?

08

1 Location expressions

Correct the wrong word in these location expressions. Check on *p.27*.

1 The sea is only six kilometres away as the pigeon flies.
2 Is the shrine inside cycling distance from here?
3 The climate is often a few degrees cooler in the coast.
4 The nearest pub is only a rock's throw from here.
5 There are shanty towns at the south of the city.
6 They live on a little farm in the centre of nowhere.
7 The capital city is fifty kilometres far from here.

8 We found an island that was **outside the beaten track**.
9 Our hotel was **right at the heart** of New York.
10 It's a **ten-minutes' walk** to the city centre.

2 Expressing preferences

Complete the second sentence so that it means the same as the first.

1 Would you rather eat out or order a takeaway?
   Which _____
2 If I could choose, I'd sooner have a room with a view of the sea.
   Given _____
3 I don't mind whether we stay a week or a fortnight.
   I'd just _____
4 I like driving better than being driven.
   I prefer _____
5 I'd rather stay in a hotel than in self-catering accommodation.
   I'd prefer _____
6 I don't mind what we do.
   I'll do _____

3 Reaching a decision

Put the lines of this dialogue in the correct order, **1** to **11**.

1	What do you reckon then, should we stay at the Ainsdale Apartments or Sandbrook Cottage?
☐	And according to the brochure, the apartments are very modern and well-equipped.
☐	Mm, me too. And I suppose we could always go and spend the day in the countryside.
☐	Yes, it does. On the other hand, the apartments would be very convenient for going out in the evening.
☐	That's a tough one, there are pros and cons in both places. Where would you rather go?
☐	That's right, I like the sound of the sauna and jacuzzi.
☐	Well, that's true, it could be a bit isolated. But, as you say, the cottage itself does sound idyllic.
☐	Yes, let's do that. I'll give them a ring now.
☐	Well, I'm not sure either. I fancy the idea of staying in a cottage but I'm not sure I like the idea of being stuck out in the middle of nowhere.
☐	Yes, we'd have everything on our doorstep. And if we're on holiday, we might as well make the most of the night life.
☐	You're right, we could hire a car and go for day trips. Maybe we should go for the apartments then.

09

1 Crime vocabulary

Complete the puzzle by following clues **1** to **10**. Find the mystery word.

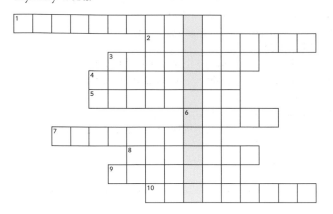

1 Juvenile _____ is becoming an increasing problem.
2 When someone has been found guilty of a crime and their conduct is monitored but they are not sent to prison, they are on _____ .
3 Someone who commits a crime is an _____ .
4 Young people who are socially _____ often turn to crime.
5 Writing or pictures on the walls of stations, public toilets, etc. is called _____ .
6 The _____ rate has risen sharply in the last year.
7 An alternative to prison is _____ service.
8 The opposite of *strict* is _____ .
9 If you are in prison awaiting trial, you are in _____ .
10 If you intentionally damage public or other people's property you _____ it.

2 Quantity expressions

Replace the words in bold with a different quantity expression with a similar meaning. Check on *p.31*.

1 Nowadays, a lot of marriages end in divorce.
2 Some species of whale are on the verge of extinction.
3 A little stress is inevitable in any job.
4 Nearly all primary school teachers are women.
5 A few children leave school unable to read or write.
6 In 99.9% of cases, there will be no problem.
7 The government is spending lots and lots of money on combating illiteracy.
8 Most young offenders come from deprived backgrounds.
9 There are hardly any pandas at all left in the wild.
10 There is a lot of evidence that poor posture causes back pain.
11 It is natural that young men will feel some aggression.
12 The violence was caused by just a handful of pupils.

3 Cause, blame, and solutions

Make complete sentences using the prompts. Check on *p.32*.

1 Main reason / teenage smoking / peer pressure.
   The main reason behind teenage smoking is peer pressure.
2 I think / something / said / banning cigarette advertising.
3 Key factor / unemployment / computerization.
4 I blame / the rise in violence / video games.
5 I think the games manufacturers / a lot / answer.
6 Reason / kids eat junk food / it is on sale at school.
7 I personally think / best way forward / create more night shelters.
8 The change in the climate / largely due / global warming.
9 The best solution / the government / introduce energy-saving measures.

10

1 Body language

Complete the expressions. Check on *p.35*.

1 clear your _____
2 raise your _____
3 clench your _____
4 shake your _____
5 cross your _____
6 tap your _____
7 snap your _____
8 blow your _____
9 rub your _____
10 fold your _____
11 tap someone on the _____
12 pat someone on the _____

2 Turn-taking

Complete the conversation using one of the expressions in the box.

can I interrupt	I've lost my train of thought
talking of	going back to
that reminds me of	sorry to interrupt
where was I	changing the subject completely
as I was saying	

Anna I had a really weird telepathic experience yesterday when I was talking to my friend. She asked me if I'd ever thought of taking up rock climbing, and ...

Bob Hey, ¹ _____ rock climbing, I've been invited to Scotland next month to go climbing. What do you think of that?

Anna Great. Fantastic. Anyway, ² _____ telepathy, my friend asked me if I'd ever thought of taking up rock climbing, and the amazing thing was that ...

Clare Hi Bob, ³ _____ but have you seen my glasses by any chance?

Bob No, sorry, I haven't. Go on, Anna. What were you saying?

Anna 4 _____ . 5 _____ ?

Bob Telepathic experiences.

Anna Oh yes. 6 _____ , it was amazing, because just before the conversation with my friend, I'd signed up for this rock climbing course in Switzerland. And I've never even discussed it with my friend.

Bob 7 _____ a cousin of mine who has a really uncanny knack of reading your mind. She knows what you're going to say before you even open your mouth.

Anna Wow. Weird, isn't it?

Bob Anyway, 8 _____ , do you fancy going out to the cinema tonight? There's a really good ...

Anna Sorry Bob, 9 _____ ? I've just spotted Clare's glasses.

11

1 Adverbs expressing attitude

Complete the text with an appropriate adverb from **1** to **8**.

The Editor
Birkdale Herald   10th October 2001

Dear Sir

I am writing to express my concern about the proposal by the town council to spend £500,000 on refurbishing the local government offices and buying a statue for the forecourt costing a further £100,000. 1 _____ , I understand the local councillors' desire for a pleasant working environment, but 2 _____ there are better ways of spending tax-payers' money?

I have made countless phone calls to the council but, 3 _____ , no one was ever available to discuss these projects. 4 _____ , they are embarrassed about the sums of money involved, and want to rush the plans through with the minimum of publicity.

If the council has £500,000 to spare, it could 5 _____ be spent in better ways. 6 _____ , there are a number of homeless people in this town, who have to sleep out on the streets in all weathers. 7 _____ , for such a large town as this, there are no facilities for offering them temporary accommodation. 8 _____ the council will reconsider their spending plans and decide to spend tax-payers' money on a more worthy cause.

Yours faithfully

Jonathan Brett

Jonathan Brett

	a	b	c
1	a ironically	b clearly	c naturally
2	a not surprisingly	b surely	c certainly
3	a strangely enough	b tragically	c fortunately
4	a clearly	b unfortunately	c amazingly
5	a fortunately	b understandably	c certainly
6	a sadly	b hopefully	c oddly
7	a obviously	b amazingly	c ironically
8	a obviously	b clearly	c hopefully

2 Uses of the definite article

Complete **1** to **12** with *the* or no article.

1 _____ telephone was invented by Alexander Graham Bell.

2 _____ friendship is more important than _____ money.

3 _____ earth revolves around _____ sun every 365 days.

4 'Where's _____ dog?' 'I think he's in _____ kitchen.'

5 _____ Internet is an important source of _____ knowledge.

6 I think _____ military service should be abolished.

7 In general, _____ dogs are more affectionate than _____ cats.

8 A quality I value highly in _____ friends is _____ loyalty.

9 _____ discovery of penicillin was one of _____ most significant medical advances.

10 _____ dove is a symbol of _____ peace all over _____ world.

11 _____ press and _____ media should respect people's right to _____ privacy.

12 He's always paying _____ compliments to _____ opposite sex.

3 Presenting an argument

Write words or phrases with a similar meaning. Check on *p.38* and *39*.

1 IN ADDITION TO THIS
  a w *hat's* _____ m *ore* _____
  b p _____ the f _____ that
  c and o _____ t _____ of t _____

2 FIRSTLY
  a f _____ of a _____
  b f _____ and f _____
  c in the f _____ p _____
  d f _____ a s _____

3 FINALLY
  a l _____
  b L _____ but n _____ l _____

4 ADMITTEDLY
  a T _____
  b Y _____
  c G _____

5 IT'S HARDLY SURPRISING THAT
  a It's s _____ surprising that
  b N _____ w _____

12

1 Feelings and moods

Unscramble the letters to make words describing moods and feelings. Check on *p.41*.

1 tedale   2 chilgrate
3 selserts
4 perisheepvan
5 loomeanit   6 steen
7 tencton
8 edidarn
9 usaxion
10 greetnice

2 Verbs of movement

Complete the sentences with the correct form of one of the verbs.

stride	dash	crawl
tiptoe	stroll	leap
wander	limp	stagger

1 She _____ into the room so as not to wake the baby.
2 Hot, thirsty, and weighed down by our heavy rucksacks, we _____ the final few yards to the youth hostel.
3 He _____ over the fence and got the ball back.
4 The centre forward _____ off the football pitch with a knee injury.
5 We _____ slowly homewards along the country lanes.
6 He dropped to his hands and knees and _____ under the table.
7 When the downpour started, we _____ to shelter under a nearby tree.
8 After they had finished the picnic, they _____ over to explore the woods.
9 The man _____ over to the reception desk and demanded to see the manager.

3 Narrative verb forms

Complete the text with a correct form of the verbs in brackets.

I [1] _____ (meet) my girlfriend when I [2] _____ (backpack) in Peru three years ago. It [3] _____ (be) the last day of my holiday. I [4] _____ (travel) for six weeks and I [5] _____ (run) out of money, so I [6] _____ (decide) to hitch the last stage of the journey. It [7] _____ (pour) with rain and I [8] _____ (carry) a heavy rucksack, so I [9] _____ (hope) that I [10] _____ (not / have to) wait too long for a lift. I [11] _____ (find) a place to wait under a tree, and [12] _____ (start) to hitch. Six hours later, I [13] _____ (still / wait). Several cars [14] _____ (go) by during the day, but nobody [15] _____ (stop). I [16] _____ (decide) to give up, and so I [17] _____ (set) off to look for a place to stay. Just then, a car [18] _____ (pull) up beside me, and a voice [19] _____ (say) 'You look a bit wet. Can I offer you a lift anywhere?' It [20] _____ (be) Justine, who is now my girlfriend.

13

1 Social situations

Write the actual words of the reported conversations.

1 Sally invited Roger to go out for a pizza, but he turned down the invitation.
   Roger, do you fancy going out for a pizza this evening?
   I'd love to but I'm afraid I'm doing something else.
2 Roger offered to help Sally with her luggage, and she accepted his offer.
3 Roger apologized profusely for being late, and Sally accepted his apology.
4 Sally asked Roger to peel the potatoes, but he refused.
5 Roger suggested Sally should go on a diet, but she rejected his suggestion.

2 Reporting verbs

Report the sentences, using an appropriate verb.

| promise | suggest | plead | tell off | deny |
| refuse | own up | urge | accuse | agree |

1 You shouldn't have borrowed my bike without asking.
2 Please don't tell my father!
3 You've broken my video recorder!
4 I didn't break your video recorder. Honestly!
5 Well, actually, I did break it.
6 I won't be late again.
7 There's no way I'm going to that party.
8 Have you thought of taking up yoga?
9 You really should see a doctor, you know.
10 OK, I'll give Sarah a ring tomorrow.

14

1 Expressions connected with lies

Choose the correct alternative for each situation.

1 The boy phoned the fire brigade even though there was no fire.
  - a It was a hoax.
  - b He was having them on.
2 She told me she loved me but really she wanted my money.
  - a She was kidding.
  - b She took me for a ride.
3 He pretended to be American, as a joke.
  - a He was taking me in.
  - b He was pulling my leg.
4 I told her I enjoyed the meal so as not to offend her.
  - a I made out she was a good cook.
  - b I told a white lie.
5 He pretended to be a policeman, and stole her passport.
  - a He tricked her.
  - b He was having her on.
6 He asked for money, even though he had plenty of his own.
  - a He was economical with the truth.
  - b He made out he needed money.

2 Proverbs

Find and correct the wrong word in the proverbs. Check on *p.48*.

1 Every cloud has a silver heart.
2 It takes all kinds to make a world.
3 All work and no pay makes Jack a dull boy.
4 When in Rome, eat as the Romans do.
5 Don't count your ducks before they are hatched.
6 Out of sight, out of memory.
7 The test of the pudding is in the eating.
8 Better now than never.
9 More haste, more speed.
10 Too many cookers spoil the broth.

3 Clarification

Write expressions under the headings. Check on *p.49*.

Asking for clarification	Providing clarification

15

1 Verb / noun collocations

Complete the sentences using an appropriate verb or multi-word verb. Check on *p.51*.

1 We are trying to design a system that will _____ everybody's needs.
2 Global warming _____ a challenge to the developed countries to consume less energy.
3 It is not easy to _____ this dilemma.
4 At the age of sixty-five he finally _____ his ambition to sail around the world single-handed.
5 The government's first priority is to _____ the problem of unemployment.
6 How much will it cost to actually _____ this scheme?
7 During the meeting, someone _____ the question of money.
8 The design team _____ several proposals during the meeting.
9 After six hours of negotiations, the two sides finally _____ an agreement.
10 I give the orders; your job is simply to _____ them _____ .

2 Putting forward proposals

Complete the suggestions for solving traffic problems in your town.

1 Some people have proposed that …
2 I suggest that …
3 It is essential that …
4 We need …
5 The council should …
6 We shouldn't …

3 Emphatic sentences with *what*

Make the sentences emphatic by starting them with *what*.

1 I bought a new car
  What I did was buy a new car
2 You should get your car serviced.
3 I need a holiday.
4 He said that he was tired.
5 We are destroying the environment.
6 We shouldn't exacerbate the problem.
7 The use of pesticides should be banned.
8 I haven't renewed my passport.
9 I'm concerned about the exhaust fumes.
10 We need to look at the cause of the problem.
11 We are simply treating the symptoms.

16

1 Talking about plans

Complete the exchanges about future plans using the prompts.

1 A you / do / weekend?

  B arranged / bowling / Saturday night. Sunday / visit / my parents / as usual. evening / revise / my exam.

2 A plans / this evening?

  B hoping / concert / but / cancelled. might / film / instead.

3 A you / anything / lined up / summer?

  B thinking / go / Greece / fortnight. after that / start new job.

2 Changes of plan

Complete the sentences with one of the multi-word verbs in the right form.

call off	talk someone out of	go through with
fall through	bring forward	get out of
pull out	stick with	

1 I was going to move house at the end of the month, but my buyers decided to _____ at the last minute.

2 The wedding was _____ because the bride got cold feet.

3 The council had been planning to build a new concert hall, but the scheme _____ for lack of sponsorship.

4 If I can _____ doing overtime, I'll meet you for a drink tonight.

5 I was having second thoughts about the colour scheme, but in the end I decided to _____ turquoise and gold.

6 If you decide you don't want to _____ the deal, let us know as soon as a matter of urgency.

7 You're not going to _____ me _____ piercing my nose. My mind's made up.

8 The meeting will be _____ so that everyone can be present.

17

1 Compound nouns for towns

Think of compound nouns to match the definitions. Check on *p.58*.

1 A place where musicians play.

2 An indoor area containing electronic games.

3 A safe place to cross the road.

4 An area of town where you can only walk on foot.

5 Where the household waste ends up.

6 A place where you can park your car.

7 Where you put your money when you park on the street.

8 A place where you can do different sports and free time activities.

9 An indoor place where there are a lot of shops together.

10 An area where a number of houses were built at the same time.

2 Two-part expressions

Unscramble the letters to make two-part expressions. Check on *p.58*.

1 dirpe and yoj

2 ciks and derit

3 cashe and spain

4 feas and donus

5 arew and rate

6 sleur and gutrailosen

7 lirat and rorer

8 evig and kate

9 scaft and sugrife

10 derit and detest

3 Talking about change

Complete the sentences with an appropriate word or phrase to describe changes.

1 There _____ to be deer in the woods.

2 The streets are no _____ safe at night.

3 There _____ used to be litter in the streets.

4 The city centre didn't _____ to be so congested.

5 You can't paddle in the sea any _____ .

6 They've _____ an amusement arcade in the centre of the town.

7 The village green has been _____ into a car park.

8 The old windmill has been _____ .

9 All the elm trees have been _____ .

18

1 Personal characteristics

Match the adjective to the descriptions.

a	thick-skinned	e	single-minded	i	self-sufficient
b	ruthless	f	cautious	j	down-to-earth
c	conscientious	g	self-effacing	k	sullen
d	obstinate	h	caring	l	stand-offish

1 She's modest and doesn't make an effort to impress people.

2 He can act cruelly, with no regard for the feelings or lives of other people.

3 He is cold and distant, and doesn't like to mix with other people.

4 She is rarely cheerful, and communicates her bad mood with silence.

5 He always fulfils his duties carefully and properly.

6 He is too insistent on doing what he wants, and no one can persuade him to do otherwise.

7 She always thinks and acts practically, without having her head in the clouds.

8 He knows exactly what he wants to do and nothing can deter him from his plan.

9 She never acts spontaneously, and generally opts for a safe course of action.

10 He is not easily hurt or offended by what others say about him.

11 She is affectionate, and tries to help and look after other people as much as she can.

12 She can manage her life without the help of other people.

2 Similarities and differences

Rewrite the sentences using the KEY words. Check on *p.62*.

1	Your salary is exactly the same as mine.	DIFFERENCE
2	Anna is much more ambitious than Tom.	NOWHERE NEAR
3	Sophie and Ellen are equally intelligent.	JUST
4	The new boss is nothing like as patient as the old one.	INFINITELY
5	I have nothing whatsoever in common with my brother.	DIFFERENT
6	Scotland is rainier than Italy.	IN COMPARISON
7	Janet and I are equally well-qualified.	IDENTICAL
8	Today is a little less cool than yesterday.	SLIGHTLY

3 Agreeing and disagreeing

Write as many expressions as you can under the headings. Check on *p.63*.

Agreeing	Disagreeing	Half agreeing

19

1 Collocations

Complete the extreme expressions. Check on *p.65*.

1	_____ idle	6	_____ new
2	_____ awake	7	_____ hot
3	_____ naked	8	_____ open
4	_____ dry	9	_____ cold
5	_____ asleep	10	_____ wet

2 Describing extreme feelings and experiences

Complete the expressions. Check on *p.65*.

1 Dad was absolutely livid. He nearly _____ the roof.

2 It was so funny. I couldn't keep a _____ face.

3 I was really embarrassed. I'll never _____ it down.

4 I was absolutely speechless. I couldn't believe my _____ .

5 It frightened the life out of me. I was absolutely _____ .

6 It was a really weird experience. In fact it was totally _____ .

7 When my team won the championship I was over the _____ .

8 It was such a devastating experience that I felt like _____ into tears.

9 When I heard that strange noise last night I felt scared _____ .

20

1 Complaining politely

Put the lines of the dialogue in order.

- [ ] Absolutely positive, I've been through all the instructions three times.
- [ ] Certainly. Have you got your receipt?
- [1] Good morning. Can I help you?
- [ ] Actually, I was rather hoping for a refund.
- [ ] Well, if you like we can give you a replacement and you can try with that.
- [ ] I see. If you could just bear with me a minute, I'll check with the manager. ...Yes, that's fine. We can issue you with a refund.
- [ ] Oh dear, what exactly is the problem?
- [ ] Actually, I can't seem to find it.
- [ ] When I press 'print' on my computer, nothing happens.
- [ ] Oh dear. I'm afraid it's our policy not to give refunds without a receipt.
- [ ] Thank you very much. I do appreciate that, and sorry for the inconvenience.
- [ ] Yes, good morning. I bought this printer here yesterday and it doesn't seem to be working.
- [ ] Are you sure it's connected properly?
- [ ] Yes, I do understand. I don't suppose there's any way you could make an exception, is there? The thing is, I've decided I might as well stick with my old printer instead of getting a new one.

2 Explaining problems

Explain a problem you might have with these appliances.

1 A computer

2 A car

3 A toilet

4 A camera

5 A TV set

6 Central heating

3 Tentative language

Rewrite the sentences using *seem* to make them less direct.

1 The radiator is leaking.
2 The battery is flat.
3 The flash doesn't work.
4 I can't set the alarm.
5 It isn't recording.
6 The colour has run.
7 They have shrunk.
8 You haven't loaded the film properly.

21

1 Expressions connected with films

Find ten words connected with films, from left to right, top to bottom, or diagonally.

```
F A R C R E D I T S
L D L E U A C K E C
O A A G V C A E N R
P P T R A I L E R E
C T G N I T E D T E
E A S C O R E W A N
R T S C L O S E U P
N I H T E I P I T L
B O X O F F I C E A
O N A S W O N G R Y
```

2 Adjectives to describe films

Complete the sentences with an adjective to describe films. Check on *p.71*.

1 It got rave reviews but, personally, I didn't think much of it; I felt it was rather _____ .

2 I like _____ films like that, that you can discuss for a long time afterwards over a drink.

3 There was nothing new or original about the plot; in fact, it was pretty _____ .

4 I prefer films with a lot of action; this one was a bit _____ for me.

5 My friend liked all the happy reunions and weddings at the end, but frankly, I found it all a bit too _____ .

6 It was a very _____ film; there were no laughs or light moments, and the ending was unbearably sad.

7 I was almost in tears when that child got out of her wheelchair and walked again; it was a very _____ scene.

8 I like the way the director didn't make the point too strongly; everything was really _____ .

9 I couldn't take my eyes off the screen from start to finish; I found the whole film very _____ .

3 Talking about films

Complete the dialogue with appropriate questions.

A ¹ _____ ?
B Yes, I saw *Titanic* the other day.
A Oh, really. ² _____ ?
B Oh, it's a typical Hollywood blockbuster.
A ³ _____ ?
B Actually, I thought it was a bit sentimental. It's not really my kind of film.
A ⁴ _____ ?
B Kate Winslet and Leonardo DiCaprio.
A ⁵ _____ ?
B Yes, they acted quite well, I thought.
A ⁶ _____ ?
B It's basically about these two people who fall in love on a sinking ship.
A ⁷ _____ ?
B No, not really, because the Leonardo DiCaprio character dies in the water waiting to be rescued.

22

1 Recent activities

Write true sentences to describe your recent activities.

1 sport
I haven't been doing much sport recently.
I've played golf twice recently / I went skiing last month.
2 cinema
3 letters / e-mails
4 jogging
5 sleep
6 cooking
7 parties
8 English
9 work
10 friends

2 Vague language

Complete the sentences using one of the expressions in the box.

such and such	and things like that	whatsisname
-ish	in his late twenties	or something
that kind of thing	or so	

1 I did a lot of sightseeing, you know, museums, art galleries, _____ .

2 You know my cousin. He's dark, _____ , got a beard.

3 There must have been fifty _____ people at the meeting.

4 Would you like a beer _____ ?

5 Can you come round at ten _____ tomorrow morning?

6 I bumped into _____ at Chris's exhibition.

7 I'm in charge of answering the phone, making reservations, dealing with customers, _____ .

8 She always has some excuse or other; 'Oh sorry, I can't make it, I'm doing _____ tonight.'

23

1 Multi-word expressions

Complete the sentences with an expression from the box.

keep track of	take issue with	give rise to
come to terms with	take charge of	make fun of
take advantage of	get the hang of	take stock of
make the best of		

1 In the absence of Mr James, Mrs Livesey will _____ the day-to-day running of the business.

2 Reversing round corners is difficult at first but you'll soon _____ it.

3 All the other kids will _____ me if I go to school wearing this!

4 She's finding it hard to _____ the fact that her children have grown up.

5 Overwork can _____ stress.

6 Now is the time to _____ the opportunities that e-commerce can offer.

7 If you try and _____ what you spend each month, you shouldn't run up debts.

8 I'm afraid I _____ your description of my novels as 'boring and dated'.

9 I know the hotel is awful, but we can't change now so we'll just have to _____ it.

10 After two years in the job, she felt it was time to _____ her career.

2 Verb phrases with *will* or the infinitive

Change the sentences to make others with a similar meaning, using the KEY word. Check on *p.78*.

1 I'm certain that you'll get the job.   BOUND
2 Petrol prices may go up.   CHANCE
3 It's unlikely that there'll be a recession.   DOUBT
4 I expect it will be warmer tomorrow.   LIKELY
5 The treaty may well be ratified.   CHANCES
6 There's no way that it will snow tomorrow.   BOUND

3 Future time expressions

Put these expressions into two groups: near time and distant time.

in five years' time	in the near future
in the coming decade	one day
by the middle of the century	in the distant future
in the next few years	within a decade or so
not in the foreseeable future	not in my lifetime

24

1 Past conditionals

Complete the sentences in an appropriate way.

1 If I hadn't gone to the party …
2 If I'd known it was your birthday …
3 You wouldn't have missed the bus if …
4 You might have got better grades if …
5 I wouldn't be feeling so sick if …
6 If we hadn't taken an umbrella …
7 He would never have known the truth if …
8 I'd be a lot richer if …

2 Expressing regret and lack of regret

Use the prompts to imagine regrets or lack of regrets for these people.

1 CHILD AFTER A VISIT TO THE ZOO
I'm glad / lions
liked / longer

2 PERSON WHOSE HOUSE HAS BEEN BURGLED
It only / burglar alarm
Thank goodness / police

3 COUPLE HOSTING A PARTY
needn't / food
just as well / wine

4 PERSON BACK FROM A HOLIDAY IN CHINA
regret / photographs
luckily / able / the Great Wall

5 PERSON WHO HAS JUST HANDED IN HER RESIGNATION
no regrets / decision
pity / sooner

6 PERSON WHO HAS JUST HAD A JOB INTERVIEW
hindsight / should / questions
wish / nervous

3 Discourse markers

Complete **1** to **10** and **a** to **j** with a preposition and find pairs of phrases. Check on *p.82*.

1 ____ first		a ____ practice
2 ____ the time		b ____ reality
3 ____ the short term		c ____ the flesh
4 ____ public		d ____ the other
5 ____ screen		e ____ private
6 ____ the surface		f ____ the long term
7 ____ normal circumstances		g ____ the current situation
8 ____ the one hand		h deep ____
9 ____ paper		i ____ the end
10 ____ theory		j ____ retrospect

WRITING

A personal profile and CV

PROFILE OF TESSA ADAMS

Personal qualities

I am a motivated, dynamic individual with ambition to succeed. I am well-organized and have good time
5   management skills; I can work to deadlines, and cope calmly under pressure. I am a good team member; I also have a proven track record of successful leadership of groups, and can delegate effectively. Articulate and approachable, I possess excellent interpersonal skills,
10 am a good listener, and at the same time I can handle problems with tact and sensitivity. Resourceful, creative, and flexible, I am an original thinker, I can take initiative, and I welcome new challenges that develop my abilities and extend my expertise.

15 **Key skills**

- I am fluent in French, and have a basic working knowledge of Italian and Finnish.
- I am highly computer-literate with an in-depth knowledge of computer graphics.
20 - Over a twelve-year period I have built up a sound understanding of the television industry.

1 Read the profile. Who do you think it describes, and why?
- a Newspaper Editor
- a PA to an accountant
- an Advertising Executive

2 Find words or phrases that mean ...
1 able to organize time well.
2 to complete work on time.
3 able to work well with other people.
4 evidence of past success.
5 to pass on work to other people.
6 able to express your ideas clearly.
7 to take action independently.
8 able to use computers.

3 Look at part of a CV. Would you set it out in the same way in your country?

CURRICULUM VITAE

Name Anthony James Corrigan

Education and qualifications

1995 – 1996 University of Bath Business School
5 Postgraduate diploma in Business management
1991 – 1995 University of Leeds
Second class Honours degree in Economics with French
I spent the year 1993 – 1994 studying French at the University of Grenoble
10 **1984 – 1991** Greenbank Comprehensive School, Harrogate
3 'A' levels: History (A), French (B), Mathematics (B)

Employment to date

2000 – present Deputy Manager, ABC Supermarket
15 15, Oxley Road, Southport PR8 4LY
1998 – 2000 Assistant Manager, Brough's Chemist's
19, Canning Road, Oxford OX2 6JE
1996 – 1998 Trainee Manager, Brough's Chemist's
Birkbeck Centre, Nottingham NG1 4ZH

4 The following headings can also be included in a CV.
1 Which would you include in your own CV?
2 Are there any you would prefer not to include? Why?

Address	E-mail address
Telephone	Sex
Nationality	Marital status
Publications	Date of birth
Interests	References

5 Write your own personal profile and CV.

Remember

- In a profile, highlight your key characteristics and skills. Use a range of expressions, e.g. *I am a ... and ... individual. / I possess good / excellent ... skills. / I have a basic / sound / in-depth knowledge / understanding of ...* .
- In a CV, list your qualifications and work experience starting with the most recent.
- Use headings, etc. to make the sections stand out.
- Your CV should be no more than one or two pages long.

An argument

Not such a great day out?

'Come and have a great day out at the zoo,' the advertisements urge. Most major towns and cities have their own municipal zoo, and most of us can remember childhood expeditions to go and throw fish to the sea-lions, crane our necks to admire the giraffes, and laugh at the antics of the penguins. Yet how much fun do zoos really provide?

There are, of course, many arguments in favour of zoos. They provide us with the opportunity to observe in the flesh animals that we could never possibly hope to view in the wild. It is also commonly argued that zoos fulfil a conservation function, by allowing the safe and selective breeding of endangered species. And last but not least, they serve an entertainment purpose, supplying us with an alternative to fairgrounds and museums as destinations for family outings.

However, the facts reveal a different side to the story. One has only to compare the pitifully short lifespans of animals kept in captivity with those of animals living in the wild to realize that a large proportion of zoo-kept animals are literally dying of unhappiness. Moreover, studies have revealed that a number of captive animals also display psychotic behaviour; polar bears in London Zoo, for example, have been observed to pace up and down in their enclosures, a behaviour pattern totally unknown in their natural habitat.

There are further compelling arguments against zoos. The contention that zoos can help conserve endangered species is surely refuted by the unsuccessful attempts in recent years to mate the last few existing zoo-kept pandas, and by the appallingly low survival rates of animals born in captivity. And as for the so-called entertainment purpose, how many of us have gone away from zoos feeling slightly ashamed, with an ill-defined sense that we have somehow been complicit in perpetuating the animals' state of captivity? Feeling that we haven't, perhaps, had such a great day out after all?

The fact is that there are, nowadays, a number of more humane alternatives to zoos. We could, for example, take our children to safari parks, where animals can at least roam free and uncaged in a much larger area. We could, in addition, encourage them to watch the excellent wildlife programmes that are widely shown on our TV screens, and support the conservation work that is being carried out in game reserves in the animals' natural habitats. In this way we could help foster a love of animals, without needing to keep them prisoner in the sad, cramped, out-dated prisons that continue to masquerade as places of entertainment.

1 Read the argument and answer the questions.
   1 Is the writer for or against zoos?
   2 What points does she include to support her argument?

2 Look at the first sentences of each paragraph. What is their purpose?

3 Identify examples of the following features.
   1 An engaging first sentence.
   2 The use of questions to involve the reader.
   3 A thought-provoking final sentence.
   4 Colourful details.
   5 Examples to support the argument.
   6 Linking words to help the flow of the argument.

4 Underline any other useful words or expressions for writing an argument.

5 Write an argument on one of the following topics.
   • Tourism
   • Cloning and genetic engineering
   • Violence on television
   • Exams

Remember
- Follow the pattern of: Introduction / Acknowledgement of opposing arguments / Explanation of your own views / Conclusion.
- Start a new paragraph for each new section, and preview the content of the paragraph in the first sentence.
- Use linking words, e.g. *First of all ...*, *Moreover ...*, *Another argument is ...*, *Finally, ...* but do not over-use these.
- Give examples and details to back up your argument.
- Make the writing more colourful by including engaging first and last sentences, specific details, and questions.

A personal letter

Sydney, 12th April 2001

Dear Seraina,

1 _____ . It sounds like you've been having a
tough time recently, and I'm sorry to hear about you and Phil
5 breaking up. I hope things are getting easier now.

2 _____ . I'm still working at U.L.P. It's hard
to believe I've been there for almost three years. Where
does the time go? Work is OK but, as you might expect, it
takes up more of my time than it should. I'm doing a lot of
10 overtime, which is quite tiring. Still, the job is secure, the
pay is good, and I get on with the people I work with.

3 _____ . I've been to Bali twice this year, and
in August, I went to the States with Melanie. This Christmas
the plan is to head back to Indonesia, with Melanie and a
15 couple of other people, but this time it'll be to Lombok,
which is supposed to be more like how Bali was fifteen years
ago, before too much development got hold of the place. I'm
really looking forward to it.

4 _____ . There are always lots of social
20 occasions to keep me busy in the evenings, but recently I've
been making more of the daytime as well, and getting out and
about exploring Sydney. I've also taken up surfing, and have
become quite obsessive about it! Not that I'm any good at
it, but life tends to revolve around the beach in summer, and
25 it's a great way of meeting new people.

5 _____ . I am British, after all! I look at the
daily forecast for the UK, and then everything about Sydney
seems OK with me! I haven't been back to England for two
years now, and quite frankly the thought of going back to
30 those long dark days and the damp cold does tend to put me
off ...

6 _____ . Mum and Dad are keeping in good
health, and are planning to come out for a visit in the new
year after Dad retires. Jenny is on the point of handing in her
35 notice and starting up a fish farm. I hope things work out for
her.

7 _____ . To be honest, I still don't know how
much longer I'll stay here in Sydney. My contract runs out in
March, and it will be decision time for me about whether to
40 stay here or move on. I like it here but I'm getting itchy feet.
Ideally, I'd like to take a year out travelling in South
America, but I'm not sure how feasible that is financially.
We'll see how things turn out.

8 _____ . How are you? Have you finished your
45 dissertation yet? How's the new job going? I hope you find
time to drop me a line with your news. I'd love to hear from
you. Take care.

Much love

Tim

---

1 Read the letter quickly.
  1 What do you think is the relationship between Tim and
    Seraina? Why?
  2 Do you think Tim is happy with his life in Australia? Why /
    why not?

2 Read the letter again.
  1 What is the topic of each paragraph?
  2 Choose a suitable first sentence (or sentences) for each
    paragraph.

  a So what can I tell you about me?
  b I suppose I should mention the weather.
  c Sorry I haven't written for so long.
  d It seems ages since I last heard from you.
  e On the whole, life goes on much the same as ever.
  f My family are doing well.
  g And what about the future?
  h I often think of you and wonder what you're up to.
  i Travel is still a passion for me.
  j Well, I've covered just about everything now, I think.
  k When it comes to free time, I try to make the most of the
    weekends.

3 Group these ways of closing a letter into two categories,
  close and more distant, according to the relationship of
  writer and receiver.

| Kind regards | Yours | Love | Lots of love |
| All my love | All the best | Best wishes | With love |

4 Underline any other words or expressions that could be
  useful when writing a personal letter.

5 Write a letter to a friend in which you describe your
  current life, recent activities, and future plans.

> **Remember**
> - You needn't write your or your friend's address at the top,
>   but it is customary to write the town and date.
> - Start the letter with *Dear* ... . Don't say *Dear friend*, ...
> - Respond to news by saying, *I'm glad / sorry to hear
>   that ..., It sounds as if ...* .
> - Start each paragraph with a suitable opening sentence.
> - Finish with an appropriate informal expression, e.g.
>   *Love* ... .
> - If you have forgotten to mention something, you can
>   include it at the end of the letter with *PS*, e.g. *PS Give my
>   regards to Chris.*

E-mails

1 Hi Claudia
This is just to confirm my flight details. I'll be arriving at Heathrow Terminal 3 at 16.45 (Flight No. BM 310). ¹ Hope to see you soon!
Alex

2 Dear Anna
Here's the agenda, as requested. ² Any comments or suggestions? ³ Meeting starts 2.15 in the Adderbury Room.
Kind regards
Paul

3 Just a reminder that we need the report on Fischer Mendel ASAP. ⁴ Any chance you could get it to me by 4.00? Sorry to rush you. Also, could you phone Colin in IT urgently re your password, as it's about to expire.
Neil

4 Dear All
I attach details of your shifts for next month. Please can you check carefully and get back to me if there are any problems.
Thanks everybody!
Mary Sanderson

5 Hello James
I'm afraid I won't be able to make lunch tomorrow. Would Weds be OK?
Harriet

6 Hi there!
Thanks for your phone message. Sorry I haven't been in touch for so long – I've been laid up with flu. Seem to be on the mend, though. ⁵ No major news. We should hear any day about the house, so we're keeping our fingers crossed. BTW have you heard from Mum recently? Have been trying to phone her but no luck. Is she away?? Hope all is well with you.
Love, Jess

a Neil, sorry about the report. ⁶ Everything a bit frantic here! I'll pull out all the stops and get it to you hopefully by 5 p.m. today. Haven't been able to get through to Colin, but will keep trying.
Peter

b Sure, no problem. Shall I pick you up one-ish and we can have a pub lunch? Give me a ring to confirm.
Speak soon
J.

c Dear Mary
Think you've forgotten I'm going to be away from the 18th. Can you swap me with someone else?
Thanks
Moira

d Thanks for your mail. ⁷ Will be there!

e Thanks for this. Could you make sure an item about room reservations is added? Thanks. See you at 2.15.
Peter

f Hi, ⁸ good to hear from you. Sorry about the flu, but glad to hear you're feeling better. Mum is in Ireland on a Tai Chi course, didn't she tell you ??! ⁹ Must dash. Due at work in ten mins. Keep me posted about the house. Matt says hello. Cheers, Alyson.

1 Read the twelve e-mails and match **1** to **6** with **a** to **f**.

2 Decide what the relationship is between the people in each exchange. How do you know?

3 How many different ways can you find ...
   1 to start an e-mail?
   2 to sign off?

4 Which words were missed out in the highlighted sections (**1** to **9**) in the e-mails?

5 What do these abbreviations stand for?
   Weds   p.m.   mins   ASAP   BTW

6 Underline any other useful expressions you can find for writing e-mails.

7 Write two e-mail exchanges that you might have ...
   1 with a friend
   2 in a work or study situation.

Remember

- E-mails are often no longer than one or two lines.
- Salutations are not always necessary, but *Dear ...,* is often used if you have not met the person you are writing to.
- Polite expressions such as *Looking forward to hearing from you* are only used in formal situations.
- Requests are usually stated simply, e.g. *Can / could you get back to me? Give me a ring.*
- If you are sending an attachment, say *Here is ..., I attach / I am sending as an attachment (a copy of ...).*
- Use abbreviations and remember you can often miss out words such as *I, there is, it is,* etc.

Formal letters

1

16, Acacia Avenue,
Merridale, Liverpool L18 5RE

The Manager,
Cranfield Mail Order,
5 Weston Rd,
Cranfield CN2 5LF
Customer Number 37402480

20th October, 2000

Dear Sir or Madam,

10 Re Order for a waterproof jacket

I am writing regarding an order I placed with your
company over six weeks ago for a waterproof jacket (Code
Number HY2 / 346). I have tried several times to phone
your Customer Services Department, but have either
15 received an engaged signal, or been asked to hold.

I sent off the order on September 5th, and unfortunately
the jacket has still not arrived. However, I note that my
VISA account has been debited for the amount of the
jacket (£65).

20 I would be grateful if you could look into the matter, and
dispatch the jacket as soon as possible, with an
explanation for the delay.

I look forward to hearing from you.

Yours faithfully,

25 *Agnes Beale*

Ms Agnes Beale

2

17, Walford St,
Burnfield BN8 2SA

17th April 2001

The Director,
Sea Experience,
5 12, The Promenade
Plymouth

Dear Sir or Madam

I am writing to enquire about windsurfing courses at
your sailing centre during the coming summer. I would
10 be grateful if you could send details of the dates of
courses in the month of August, along with rates and
reservation information. I would also be glad if you
could answer the following questions:

1   Do you offer special rates for families?
15 2   Is it necessary to be able to swim in order to take part
in the courses?
3   Are there any courses available for children under
seven?

I enclose a stamped addressed envelope for your reply.

20 With thanks in advance,

Yours faithfully,

Alice Stevenson

Alice Stevenson (Mrs)

3

Seaton Hall
University of Exeter,
Exeter EX4 5TB

May 3rd 2001

5 Dear Mr Evans,

I have been given your name by my college tutor, Dr
Sean O'Brady, who said you may be able to help me
with a research paper I am writing on Dylan Thomas.
I understand that you were a close friend of his, and
10 have some letters he wrote during his final years.

I wonder if it would be at all possible for me to pay you
a brief visit, and whether you might consider letting me
have a look at some of the letters? I will be visiting
Cardiff in the first week of June, and would be able to
15 call in at any time during that week that is convenient
for you. If you could write or e-mail to let me know
when I could call on you, I would be most grateful.

I do hope it will be possible to meet you.

Yours sincerely,

20 *Gustavo Espinoza*

Gustavo Espinoza

4

Sarah Gunn
Accommodation Officer
Princes Language Academy
Barry Rd
5 Oxford OX2 2KR

84, Benson Rd,
Headington,
Oxford OX3 4HU

4th March 2001

Dear Ms Gunn,

I am writing in response to your advertisement in
last Friday's Oxford Times for host families for
10 students at your language school.

My husband and I have recently retired and our
children have all left home. As a result we now have
time on our hands and would be happy to welcome a
foreign student into our home. We have a spare
15 room, which is not large, but is quite cosy. Our
house is a three-bedroom semi in a quiet residential
area, and is on a bus route to the city centre. We
could provide good home cooking and a friendly
atmosphere.

20 Do telephone us on 01865 712393 if you would like
to arrange a time to visit.

I look forward to hearing from you.

Yours sincerely

Ann McCarthy

Ann McCarthy (Mrs)

---

1 Read the four letters. In each case, decide whether the main purpose of the letter is ...
 1 to request information.
 2 to make a complaint.
 3 to make an offer.
 4 to make a request.

2 Underline expressions used ...
 1 to state the purpose of the letter.
 2 to make a request.
 3 to make a complaint.
 4 to make an offer.
 5 to request information.
 6 to say you are sending something with the letter.
 7 to finish the letter.

3 When do we use *Yours sincerely* ... and *Yours faithfully* ...?

4 Write one of the following letters.
 1 a letter to complain about problems with an airline.
 2 a letter to request information about a language school.
 3 a letter to invite someone to speak at a meeting.

Remember
- Notice the different places to write your address.
- When writing to a company, write the name, position and address of the person you are writing to.
- Open and close your letter appropriately, e.g. *Dear Sir, ... / Yours faithfully ...* .
- State the purpose of your letter at the beginning, *I am writing to enquire / complain / apply for / invite / thank* etc. *I am writing regarding / in connection with / in response to...* .
- You can state the subject of the letter using *Re* (see letter 1).
- Make polite requests, e.g. *I would be (very) grateful / glad if you could ... / I wonder if it would be possible ...? Could you please ...?*
- Finish with an expression, e.g. *I look forward to hearing from you / With thanks in advance.*

A report

REPORT ON THE FERRY ROAD CYCLE TRACK

This report has been written to inform the local community of the results of an investigation into the use of the new cycle track between Ferry Road and the city centre, which was carried out in the first week of March
5 2001.

The purpose of the investigation was to determine how successful the track has been in meeting the needs of the people in the Marston area, and to discover any problems that may have been experienced by its users.
10 Questionnaires were distributed to cyclists throughout the week. Respondents were asked to supply biographical information, and were asked for what purposes and how frequently they used the track, how satisfied they were with it, and whether they had any
15 suggestions for improving it.

It was found that the track is mainly used for the purpose of commuting to and from work, but is also used for leisure and recreation. Most users fall into the 20 – 50 age bracket, and surprisingly few schoolchildren use the
20 track. It is used on a regular basis by most people, with fewer than 10% of cyclists saying that they used it once a week or less.

The investigation also revealed that over 80% of users were satisfied with the track overall, with one in five of
25 these claiming to be very satisfied. Reasons for satisfaction centred mainly on the fact that it provided a safe alternative to car use, but a substantial number of replies mentioned the fact that it cut journey times to work, and provided a welcome escape from traffic-
30 clogged and polluted roads. Regarding improvements, one third of respondents referred to the unsatisfactory lighting at night, and a small number commented on the need for resurfacing on certain stretches of the track.

Overall, it appears that the track is fulfilling its purpose of
35 providing a safe alternative route for cyclists in the Marston area, and that the vast majority of its users are satisfied with it.

As a result of the investigation, the following recommendations have been made:

40 ● that the council should investigate the lighting and take appropriate measures to ensure that it does not fail at night.

● that resurfacing should take place on two stretches of the road.

45 ● that the Cycling Officer should liaise with local schools to encourage more children to use the track to travel to school.

---

1 Identify these sections in the report.
- Aim of report
- Background information
- Findings
- Conclusions
- Action points

2 Find and underline …
   1 examples of passive and impersonal structures.
   2 expressions used to quote statistics.
   3 other useful expressions for writing a report.

3 Write a report on an investigation into the use of a local facility, e.g. a library, youth club, or sports centre.

Remember
- Give the report an informative title.
- Follow the structure: Aim / Background information / Findings / Conclusions / Action points.
- Use sub-headings for each new section.
- Use passive and impersonal structures, e.g. *Questionnaires were distributed …, the following recommendations have been made …, It was agreed / felt / found that … .*
- Use bullet points or lists where appropriate.
- Avoid giving personal opinions.

EXTRA MATERIAL

04 SO WHAT IS IT YOU DO?

Speak out   Student A

Read your roles and check any new words in a dictionary. Ask **B** what his / her job is and say what you think it involves. Swap roles.

1 SUB-EDITOR

- You work on a magazine which gives details of the television programmes on all channels.
- You are responsible for editing the descriptions of films / programmes supplied by production companies and press offices, and for writing captions for photos.
- You have to keep to tight deadlines and you often work anti-social hours.

2 SYSTEMS ANALYST

- You work for a software company and are currently involved in a transport systems project.
- Your main role is to help people understand what a particular computer system can do so that it can be designed in the most effective way for your project.
- You work as part of a team and a lot of your time is spent liaising with other team members.

05 LOVE AT FIRST SIGHT?

Speak for yourself   Student A

Check your collocations. In pairs, ask and answer the questions.

1 Would you ever go on a **blind date**? Why / why not?
2 Do you ever read the **lonely hearts** column in the newspaper?
3 Do most people in your country see marriage as a **lifelong commitment**?
4 How would you define a **soul mate**?
5 Have you ever been / would you ever go to a **singles bar**?

05 LOVE AT FIRST SIGHT?

Reading   Student B

Read the text and make notes to answer the questions.

The air is thick with sweat, scent, and anticipation as a thousand of Berlin's loneliest hearts cram into a tent to try their luck at *Fisch sucht Fahrrad* (*Fish seeks Bicycle*), the city's most popular singles party. As they cruise along the dance floor, the men and women, most in their thirties and forties, take a discreet look at the number each one wears on their chest. Interested parties can leave messages for one another on a giant notice board, but the numbers can also identify advertisers in the lonely hearts pages of Berlin's top listings magazine, offering prospective partners the chance to make an anonymous assessment of each other's physical charms. 'It saves you the disappointment you often feel when you meet someone through an ad and it means no one has to say no to you face to face,' says Stefan, a thirty-nine-year-old office worker who admits he has been hunting for a long-term partner for over two years.

An alternative is to advertise in the paper. The city's leading tabloid runs regular profiles of 'Berlin's most eligible bachelors', with photos of melancholy looking businessmen in vast, empty flats. Most of these eligible men claim they are yearning to meet the right woman, settle down, and start a family. But many of Berlin's new breed of singles are happy the way they are and have no intention of letting love interfere with their successful, high-powered lives. 'The idea of looking at the same partner every evening bores me to tears. It's better to see each other twice a week, but intensely,' says Maria Bohne, a thirty-year-old arts administrator.

This sentiment is not shared by Norbert, who is among hundreds of singles who appear each week on *Spreckanal*, one of four television stations in the city that fill hours of airtime each day with lonely hearts videos. Norbert is forty-four, overweight, and balding, and he is waiting impatiently for Fräulein Right to come along and share his social life. 'She should have long, dark hair, and I like a woman to show her legs, so short skirts, please. And she should have a personality just like mine.'

Fish seeks bicycle The name of the venue comes from the expression 'A woman needs a man like a fish needs a bicycle'.

1 Which three ways of meeting a partner are described in the text?
2 How do Stefan, Maria, and Norbert differ in what they are looking for from a partner?

08 FARAWAY PLACES

Speak out   Student A

Read the text and highlight the points which appeal to you, things which don't appeal, and anything you are uncertain about.

POPEYE GUEST HOUSE

In a fabulous location right in the heart of Cangalute, the liveliest resort in Goa, the newly built Popeye Guest House offers simple, comfortable accommodation. All around you local life goes on and the family next door keep chickens and pigs in their back yard. It's a familiar sight to see a whole family of pigs and goats parading through the streets. This is definitely the place to mingle with the locals, and get a 'real feel' for Goan life, and the friendly hotel proprietors are renowned for their hospitality and for taking an interest in their guests. The gorgeous Cangalute beach is just a stone's throw away, and at night you can hear the waves gently lapping against the shore and the breeze whispering through the palms; perfect for early morning walks and moonlight dips. The hotel is located close to local shops, restaurants and discotheques. The guest house has its own rooftop restaurant, with homely local cuisine, and a café / bar is planned for next season. The rooms have twin bedrooms, ceiling fan, and spacious ensuite shower with hot water and WC. Great value for those on a budget.

09 CAUSE FOR CONCERN

Speak out

Read the proposed solutions for tackling the problem of juvenile crime.

1 a Invest in an early intervention scheme, whereby social workers identify children at risk of getting involved with crime.
   - How could such children be identified?
   - What would be done with the children at risk?

 b Provide more sports and recreation facilities in the town.
   - What exactly would be provided?
   - How would this help?

2 a Increase funding to the local police force, to recruit more police officers and implement a liaison scheme between the police and local schools.
   - What exactly would the police do?
   - How would this solve the problem?

 b Set up a community service system, whereby prisoners help in the community instead of going into prison.
   - What exactly could the offenders do?
   - What problems might arise and how could they be overcome?

3 a Investigate and set up a system of restorative justice, whereby young offenders are forced to confront the victims of their crime.
   - Who would administer the scheme, and what would it involve?
   - How would it help solve the problem of crime?
   - What problems might arise?

 b Invest in a job creation scheme to increase employment opportunities.
   - Who would administer and finance the scheme?
   - How would it work in practice?

11 OUR CLEVEREST INVENTION

Reading   Student B

Read the text and note down the main points that the writer uses to support his argument.

THE BOOK

The Internet is a fabulous new institution; instant, current, vast, and global. For up-to-date knowledge about the state of the world now, electronic data may represent a new and exciting way of reaching information. But the book still has a successful career ahead of it. Bear in mind that no new technology has entirely supplanted an old one.

It is scarcely surprising that we have a deep emotional attachment to the book. After all, it is the most potent artefact ever created by humanity. It is a masterpiece of design: it's virtually indestructible, portable and versatile, but above all self-contained. No expensive hardware, intervening software, password or downloading stands between the human eye and the printed page. The book can very effectively stand up for itself against electronic media.

For a wide range of uses, the book is ideal. For novels, poetry, plays, biographies; for linear reading, rather than intermittent consultation, the book is best. Books for the bed and beach, disks for details and data. And don't forget: the Internet may have grown massively, but more books are being published now than at any time in history. How's that for staying power?

The Internet has a lot going for it. So has the book, because it's still our cleverest invention, and we shall not, and need not, do without all its wonderful features.

The Guardian

Reading Student B

Read your text and find words / expressions from ex.1 on *p.56*.

I don't know if it happens the other way around, but almost everybody who lives in the city sometimes thinks of leaving it. Stuck in a traffic jam, squeezing onto the underground train, pushing a buggy at noxious exhaust-fume level along a crowded street, we imagine a more innocent world, where the horizons are wide and the air pure, where birds sing from the tree tops.

Of course, the countryside isn't natural any more; it is manufactured and tame. The forests have gone, the coasts are eroded by global warming. There is oil on the beaches, pollution in the rock pools. Farms have become agrochemical production sites, as industrial as a factory making computers. In these rural-industrial sites, the countryside has been abolished; the hedgerows where wildlife flourished have been wiped away, and pesticides have meant the death of hundreds of species of insects and birds and wild flowers. Motorways and A-roads thunder through little villages; you can be in more danger from cars on country lanes than in the towns. Whole communities have died out in the country. There are villages without shops or pubs or churches which are just commuter corridors. You can live by a farm and yet only be able to buy fresh fruit and vegetables from the huge supermarkets.

Yet I am very glad to be leaving the city. I don't want to be in the swing of things really, in the grip of fashion and speed and ambition. I won't miss the city where everything is carved up by roads and dual carriageways, and with mile upon mile of houses, factories, shops, broken windows, untended gardens, stations, industrial wastelands, great rubbish dumps, scrap yards, plastic bags flying in the dirty wind, cemeteries, and walls covered with graffiti. I dream of the sensuous and earthy smells of the countryside; wet grass, pigs, flowers, mulched leaves, the salty east wind, autumn bonfires. I long to be in the garden, sinking my fingers into the earth, getting my hands dirty at last. I imagine evenings, after work is done, when we can all drive to the coast and walk on the shingle beaches.

Maybe we'll all go mad in the country, or maybe we'll end up saner and more contented. Maybe in a year or two we'll return and be back in the crowds dreaming of escape. But maybe we won't.

The Observer

English in use Student A

Describe photo **1** to **B** and listen to their description. Discuss how you think the place has changed, using expressions from *p.59*. Then swap roles with photo **2**.

1  2

19 ABSOLUTELY UNBELIEVABLE!

Speak out Student A

Look at the photos and prepare to tell two holiday anecdotes.

1  2

20 A BIT OF A PROBLEM

Speak out Student A

Read your information and act out the telephone conversations. You have five minutes per roleplay to reach agreement. Swap roles after each one.

Roleplay 1 Phone Student **B**

You have recently had a shower installed by a local plumbing firm. A week after it was installed the water started running hot and cold. You are going to phone up to complain.

Think What do you want the firm to do? What compromise are you prepared to accept?

Roleplay 2 Student **B** phones you

You work for telephone bookings of American Airlines. You do not deal with on-line bookings.

Think How will you deal with queries about on-line bookings?

Roleplay 3 Phone Student **B**

You ordered a coat from a mail order company and it was sent to you a month ago. You have not worn it because it is too big. You want to return it, but you realize you have passed the twenty-one-day limit for returning goods. You phone the mail order company.

Think What will you say to persuade them to take back the coat?

Reading Student A

Read about the films showing at the Phoenix cinema.
Decide what kind of film each one is and underline words used to describe them.

GIRLS' NIGHT

Director Nick Hurran
Starring Brenda Blethyn, Julie Walters,
Kris Kristofferson, George Costigan
GB 1998 95 mins

Receiving a standing ovation following its premiere at the Sundance Film Festival, *Girls' Night* is a beautifully acted, genuinely moving and uplifting tale of friendship and new beginnings. Jackie and Dawn leave their monotonous factory jobs behind them every Friday when they go for a girls' night at the bingo. When Dawn wins £100,000 she shares her winnings with Jackie, giving her best friend the chance to finally leave her husband and her irksome job. For Dawn, however, her luck is overshadowed by the knowledge that she has cancer. When Jackie discovers Dawn's secret she impulsively whisks her away for a dream holiday in Las Vegas where they live it up, amongst the rhinestones and Elvis impersonators, until reality finally breaks in. With a conscious nod towards *Thelma and Louise*, *Girls' Night* cleverly steers clear of sentimental schmaltz in favour of heartfelt emotion, largely thanks to the humour and honesty of the script and powerful performances by two of Britain's best loved actresses.

POINT**BLANK**

Director John Boorman
Starring Lee Marvin, Angie Dickinson
USA 1967 92 mins

One of the definitive films of the late 60s, John Boorman's masterful adaptation of Richard Stark's *The Hunter*. Clearly influenced by Boorman's European sensibilities and bearing comparison to Godard's *Alphaville*, *Point Blank* is an enigmatic thriller, a compelling look at man in the urban jungle and crucial in the development of the cinema's portrait of America as a complex of organized crime. Lee Marvin, arguably cinema's most intensely powerful tough guy, gives his finest performance in a riveting account of a dying gangster's fantasies of wreaking revenge on the faceless criminal organization responsible for his demise in which the actual and the imaginary are perfectly joined through flashback and elliptical editing.

Celebrity

Director Woody Allen
Starring Kenneth Branagh, Leonardo
DiCaprio, Melanie Griffith, Judy Davis,
Famke Janssen, Winona Ryder, Charlize
Theron, Joe Mantegna, Vanessa
Redgrave, Hank Azaria
USA 1998 114 mins

Filling the role normally reserved for writer/director Woody Allen, Kenneth Branagh plays the neurotic lead: aspiring screen writer and would-be novelist Kee Simon, whose lack of success takes a toll on his marriage to Judy Davis. As a divorced single, he embarks on a course of serial flirtation and encounters with famous women, acquiring a literary-agent girlfriend in a determined attempt to turn his life around and gain celebrity status. A star cast includes Leonardo DiCaprio playing a tempestuous young film star and Melanie Griffith as a breezy actress. Made on a budget of only $800,000 this stylish black and white feature offers a rueful, hilarious take on the pursuit of fame and success.

Saving Private Ryan

Director Steven Spielberg
Starring Tom Hanks, Tom Sizemore,
Matt Damon, Edward Burns
USA 1998 168 mins

Savage, harrowing, and at times utterly breathtaking, *Saving Private Ryan* is Steven Spielberg at his very best. In many ways a natural progression from *Schindler's List*, the film follows six American soldiers on a secret mission through occupied France in search of a private who is to be sent home on compassionate grounds following the death of his three brothers. Reluctantly the men search for Private Ryan, frustrated that they are being sent on a PR exercise at such a crucial stage in the battle, but as the war rages around them, their determination to ensure that this is not a futile mission grows. Already, and justifiably, being hailed as one of the truly great war films, its claim rests largely on a truly stunning twenty-six-minute opening sequence of the D-Day landings, a piece of film-making of such outstanding technical virtuosity, emotional force, and palpable terror that it is difficult to imagine how anyone could commit anything more powerful to film. Simply masterful.

Elizabeth

Director Shekhar Kapur
Starring Cate Blanchett, Geoffrey Rush,
Christopher Eccleston, Joseph Fiennes,
Richard Attenborough, Fanny Ardant,
Kathy Burke, Eric Cantona, Vincent
Cassel, John Gielgud
GB 1998 122 mins

One of the most original and intriguing period dramas of recent years, *Elizabeth* is a beautifully filmed, densely woven historical thriller, which focuses on the turbulent times surrounding the accession of Princess Elizabeth to the throne and the early months which shaped her into the legendary Virgin Queen. Drawn to the script by the astonishing modernity of Elizabeth's character, *Bandit Queen* director Shekhar Kapur has created a darkly vivid tale of intrigue, conspiracy, and betrayal, revolving around a powerful performance from Cate Blanchett as the increasingly independent Elizabeth forced to make the difficult choice between personal happiness and her responsibilities as queen.

04 SO WHAT IS IT YOU DO?

Speak out   Student B

Read your roles and check any new words in a dictionary. Answer **A**'s questions about your job and swap roles.

1   INDEPENDENT FINANCIAL ADVISER
- You work for the financial services side of a private bank in the City of London.
- You are responsible for your own list of both corporate and individual clients.
- You advise on a wide range of issues including pensions, investment, and tax planning.

2   RESTAURANT MANAGER
- You work for a four-star hotel chain in one of their two hundred-seater London restaurants.
- You are reponsible for the smooth running of the restaurant as well as the training and recruitment of the kitchen and waiting staff.
- You work every evening and Sunday lunchtimes.

08 FARAWAY PLACES

Speak out   Student B

Read the text and highlight points which appeal to you, things which don't appeal, and anything you are uncertain about.

Bangaram
ISLAND RESORT

The resort is made up of thirty simple huts built in blocks of four, but we'd like to warn you that the walls are of tissue-like proportions, so that any loud neighbours will be heard by all and sundry, and could be a major source of entertainment or irritation! The rooms are simply furnished, have twin beds, telephone, ceiling fan and ensuite shower and WC, with hot water connected to the shower only. There is a dining hut by the beach, where all meals are taken in buffet style. At least once a week there is a beach barbecue, and the chef will happily cook for you any fish you've been lucky enough to catch on one of your fishing expeditions. Note that this area is well known for its fishing industry, and you can expect the occasional smell from the traditional fish drying process. After lunch you'll most likely want to have a little siesta, and one of the many hammocks suspended from the palm trees around the huts is the ideal place. Emphasis here is on natural beauty and simplicity; a paradise for sunworshippers, divers and snorkellers, and anyone who wants to get away from it all and have a relaxing 'no frills' holiday.

05 LOVE AT FIRST SIGHT?

Speak for yourself   Student B

Check your collocations. In pairs, ask and answer the questions.
1   Do you think the concept of an **eligible bachelor** still exists?
2   What do you think about **arranged marriages**?
3   Is there such a thing as **Mr** or **Ms Right**?
4   In your country, do people usually get married in church or with a **civil ceremony** in a **registry office**?

05 LOVE AT FIRST SIGHT?

Reading   Student C

Read the text and make notes to answer the questions.

Abjhit Banerji, a chartered accountant, and his wife Moona, a GP, were both born and brought up in Gerrards Cross, a wealthy suburb of London. The couple are both Hindu Bengali from similar castes, and their marriage was arranged by their parents. Moona, thirty-four, says, 'I was brought up with the idea that when I was ready to get married, if I hadn't already met somebody, I would be introduced to suitable matches. My mother always said it didn't have to be someone she found for me. But I decided I wanted to meet a partner like this, because I wanted to marry someone who was ultimately of my background and culture that I would be able to understand.' Abjhit, thirty-six, agrees. 'It never even occurred to me to go about marriage any other way. I knew instinctively that I would have to settle down with someone who shared my set of beliefs.'

The couple 'discovered' each other through the extensive Asian 'network'. A mutual friend suggested they might be compatible and put the parents in touch with each other. Then Moona, accompanied by her older brother, met Abjhit and his sister at a restaurant. 'It was a nice way of breaking the ice,' says Abjhit. 'On a traditional date, you're on your own. But we knew our families were behind us, so there was none of the initial awkwardness. The basis of the introduction is that you are meeting someone for a lifelong commitment and that is crystal clear right from the start.'

Neither felt under any pressure to feign affection or to force the match to work. Moona explains, 'The first time we met it was just to decide whether we actually wanted to speak to each other again. There was no need to flirt or chat each other up or pay compliments. If we hadn't liked each other, that would have been the end of it.'

Moona and Abjhit have no doubt that they will play an important part in the marriages of their own children. Abjhit says, 'We feel it is our duty to help our children at that momentous time of their lives when they want to settle down. That's the last thing you have to do for your children; marry them off to the right person.'

1   What are the advantages of arranged marriages mentioned in the text?
2   What was different about their first date?

08 FARAWAY PLACES

Speak out   Student C

Read the text and highlight the points which appeal to you, things which don't appeal, and anything you are uncertain about.

PARK LANE GUEST HOUSE

The Park Lane offers simple, clean accommodation just a couple of minutes' walk from the beach. A five-minute walk along the beach will take you to the nearest auto-rickshaw and taxi station where you can take a taxi to the resort centre; or, for the more energetic, it can be reached by a leisurely stroll along Lighthouse Beach. The Park Lane has a lovely courtyard decorated with cane furniture, surrounded by plants and with an overhead passion fruit trellis, where you can relax in a peaceful atmosphere with a good book, a long cool drink, and an interesting selection of local foods. Each room has its own spacious, modern bathroom, with WC and shower (cold water only). The staff are extremely friendly, and if you can't stand a cold shower, they will boil up a couple of buckets, and deliver it right to your door. A penthouse in Park Lane it's not, but what it lacks in facilities it more than makes up for in character and tranquillity, and provided you're not expecting the Ritz, we think you'll love it. Please note that access to Park Lane is by a steep uneven path followed by a five-minute walk along the beach, and is not suitable for those with walking difficulties.

17 AWAY FROM IT ALL

English in use   Student B

Listen to **A**'s description of their photo **1** and then describe your photo **1**. Discuss how you think the place has changed using expressions from *p.59*. Then swap roles with photo **2**.

19 ABSOLUTELY UNBELIEVABLE!

Speak out   Student B

Look at the photos and prepare to tell two holiday anecdotes.

20 A BIT OF A PROBLEM

Speak out   Student B

Read your information and act out the telephone conversations. You have five minutes per roleplay to reach agreement. Swap roles after each one.

Roleplay 1   Student **A** phones you

You are the manager of a small plumbing firm. All your plumbers are fully booked up for the next ten days. It is company policy to take responsibility for the work of the plumbers, but complaints about materials should be addressed to the manufacturers.

Think   How are you going to deal with emergency requests?

Roleplay 2   Phone Student **A**

You have bought a plane ticket to New York over the Internet, but you have not yet received confirmation by post of the booking. You are anxious, because the flight is tomorrow. You are going to phone American Airlines.

Think   What exactly do you want from the airline?

Roleplay 3   Student **A** phones you

You are the customer relations officer for a mail order clothing company. Your policy is not to accept returned goods after 21 days.

Think   How far are you prepared to bend company policy for the sake of good customer relations?

Reading Student B

Read about films showing at the Phoenix cinema.
Decide what kind of film each one is and underline words used to describe them.

My Name is Joe

Director Ken Loach
Starring Peter Mullan, Louise Goodall,
David McKay, Annemarie Kennedy,
David Hayman
UK 1998 105 mins

Despite often having the reputation for being worthy and a tad depressing, Ken Loach's films are distinguished by a warmth and genuine love of humanity, ensuring that they are, in reality, surprisingly uplifting in their celebration of human strength, resilience, and wry humour. Much of the heart of his latest film, *My name is Joe*, lies in the performance and charisma of Peter Mullan, who justifiably won the award for Best Actor at Cannes for his portrayal of a charming, unemployed, lonely man whose main love is coaching a particularly talentless football team. He glimpses a new and potentially better life when he meets Sarah, a social worker involved with some of his football team. As they gradually come together, the realities and complications of life both bind them and threaten to split them up. Gritty, honest and compelling, the film's passion, warmth and life sweep you along to the heartbreaking devastating ending. Simply marvellous.

Tea with Mussolini

Director Franco Zefferelli
Starring Joan Plowright, Judi Dench,
Maggie Smith, Cher, Lily Tomlin,
Michael Williams
Italy / GB 1998 117 mins

With delightful performances from an impressive cast, *Tea with Mussolini* is the gentle, moving, and beautiful tale of a group of rather eccentric expatriates determined to remain in Florence as Italy heads towards war. In the midst of their world, the group meet for tea every day, attempting to maintain a little corner of Britain, with complete, if deluded, faith that Mussolini will protect them. Renowned for visual splendour in his films, legendary Italian director Franco Zefferelli has captured the delicate beauty of the Tuscan landscapes as well as the determination of a group of British ladies.

A Simple Plan

Director Sam Raimi
Starring Bill Paxton, Billy Rob
Thornton, Bridget Fonda
USA 1998 121 mins

A tense, psychological thriller set in snowy Minnesota, which earned Academy Award nominations for best supporting actor and best screenplay based on previously published material. Brothers Hank (Thornton) and Jacob (Paxton) come across a plane wreckage in their local woods and find $4.4 million in cash. They decide to keep the money and agree to split it when the snow thaws. While one brother wants to keep the money, the other struggles with his conscience and a string of blunders bring the police on the trail. A gripping tale of greed, paranoia, and distrust from *Evil Dead* director Sam Riami.

North *by* Northwest

Director Alfred Hitchcock
Starring Cary Grant, Eva Marie Saint,
James Mason
USA 1959 136 mins

Opening with Saul Bass' snappily funny credits sequence, the delightful comic-thriller *North by Northwest* is perhaps Alfred Hitchcock's most perfectly realized film. Cary Grant gives one of his finest performances as the self-satisfied, suave ad exec who is mistaken for a spy and finds himself pursued by enemy agents convinced that he knows too much. Based on a script by Ernest Lehman, it is the quintessential chase movie and a compendium of its director's cinematic trademarks; ingenious shots, subtle male-female relationships, a dramatic score by Bernard Herrmann, bright technicolour insider jokes, witty symbolism, and masterly orchestrated suspense. Interweaving themes of paranoia, isolation, and sexual anxiety with responsibility and redemption, the film is a bizarre tightrope between sex and repression, nightmarish thriller and urban comedy.

eXistenZ

Director David Cronenberg
Starring Jennifer Jason, Jason Leigh,
Jude Law, Willem Dafoe, Ian Holm
USA 1999 96 mins

Smoothly blending horror and black humour, David Cronenberg returns to more familiar territory after *Crash*, with his first original screenplay since *Videodrome*. In a not too distant future, a group of people assemble for a seminar to test a computer game and meet its designer, Allegra (Leigh). Minutes into the first game, a member of the audience pulls out a gun and fires, wounding Allegra, who escapes with a security guard (Law). Disconcerting, playfully absurd, and great fun.

TRAINSPOTTING

Director Danny Boyle
Starring Ewan McGregor, Ewen
Bremmer, Jonny Lee Miller, Kevin
McKidd, Robert Carlyle, Kelly
MacDonald
GB 1995 91 mins

The *Shallow Grave* team's hilarious but harrowing screen adaptation of Irvine Welsh's powerful, comic, cult novel. Capturing the surreal tone of the book and using much of its obscenity splattered language, *Trainspotting*, whilst acknowledging the terrible, destructive side of drugs, is about the decision to choose life. Intense, bleak, horribly realistic, and very, very funny.

TAPESCRIPTS

01 NICE TO MEET YOU

1 Excuse me. Is anybody sitting here?
   I'm afraid it's taken, actually.
2 Have you been waiting long?
   No, only about ten minutes.
3 Mind if I join you?
   Go ahead.
4 Do you know when the next bus is due?
   In about half an hour I think.
5 Lovely weather!
   Yeah, beautiful, isn't it?
6 Have you got change for a fiver by any chance?
   I haven't I'm afraid. I'm sorry.
7 Have you got the time?
   I make it twenty to.
8 These trains are always late, aren't they?
   Yeah, they're not very punctual, are they?

1
A Ah! Henry. Allow me to introduce Ed Bamber. Ed's
   in charge of our overseas division. Ed, this is
   Henry Goodfellow, who's just joined us from ICI.
B How do you do.
C Nice to meet you.

2
A Do you two know each other?
B I don't think so …
C No, I don't think we've met, have we?
A Tim, this is Louise. Louise, Tim.
B Hi. Nice to meet you.
C Yeah, you too.
A Tim's just spent three years travelling around the
   world.
C Ah, a globe-trotter.
B Yeah, that's right, I …

3
A Sarah, have you met Philippa? Philippa and I used
   to share a house together.
B Actually, your face looks familiar. But I don't think
   we've actually spoken, have we?
C Yeah, you look familiar too. Where do I know you
   from?
B Mmm. You don't play badminton?
C No …

4
A Angela, can I introduce Ingrid, an ex-colleague of
   mine at Pegasus?
B We're old friends, actually.
C Yes, Angela and I were at school together.

5
A Excuse me. Can I introduce myself? My name's
   Clare Hardy. I'm doing a research project on Ted
   Hughes, and I understand you've just written a
   book on him?
B Oh, yes, that's right.
A Well, I was wondering …

6
A Hi, I'm Naomi.
B Hi, I'm Tom.

A Great party.
B Yeah.
A Can I get you a drink?
B Oh, thanks. Gin and tonic, please. With ice.

02 TIME FLIES

1
Well, the thing is, it takes me about, erm, two hours
each way on the train and then another twenty
minutes on the underground, so by the time I get
home in the evening after a full day's work, I'm
completely exhausted and, er, really don't feel like
doing anything, apart from having something to eat
and then collapsing in front of the TV. I don't do any
sport and I hardly ever go out during the week.

2
I have to get up really early to get Jo, my eldest,
ready for nursery, and at the same time make sure
that Sophie is all right and that she gets some
breakfast. So, by the time I've taken Jo to nursery on
the bus and then come back and dropped Sophie off
at the childminder round the corner, it's already
about 9.30 and then I have to rush to get into work
by 10.00. And, er, in the afternoon it's pretty much
the same thing in reverse order and by the time the
kids are in bed, I'm ready to fall asleep myself.

3
I get up at about 6.30 because my school's a long
way from where I live and I have to get the bus. And
then I get home from school at about 5.00, watch a
bit of TV if I'm lucky, and have to start doing my
homework. I usually get about two hours' homework
a night, so if I don't start by 6.00, it's difficult to
finish in time and have supper and be in bed by 9.30.
I wish I could see my friends in the evenings but
there just isn't enough time.

03 FOOD FOR THOUGHT

A
It just seems to me that children these days don't get
a balanced diet any more and they grow up with all
sorts of health problems as a result. And schools have
got a lot to answer for; they offer far too much
choice in their canteens without actually educating
the kids. And far too much junk food on the menu
and you'll find a lot of the kids just going for that, so
all they're getting is fat and sugar with no guarantee
that they'll get a decent evening meal.
And then, if they take packed lunches, you find that
parents will give them crisps and chocolate and fizzy
drinks anyway, so they're no better off. I mean, I'm
not saying that it's better to be force-fed school
dinners like I was but there must be some way of
making sure these kids at least know what a
balanced diet is.

B
You see these images of families in the old days, you
know, all sitting round the table, um, er, the kids
eating what they're given because that's all there
was. Um, everyone eating the same food at the same
time and actually talking to each other sometimes.
Um, you know, sometimes that's pretty unusual in my
family unless it's a special occasion. Er, there'll be my
eldest watching the telly in the lounge with her
dinner on her lap, um, er, there's my youngest lying
on the floor upstairs watching something else. Um,
and then my husband tends to come in quite late so
he hardly ever eats at the same time as the rest of
us.
Oh, and life would be a lot simpler if they'd all eat
the same things without complaining about it all the
time. Oh, honestly, I tend to end up cooking three
different meals, yeah, either Sara's on a diet or off
eating this and that or Josh is going through one of
his phases of only eating chips and beans. You know,
and then my husband always wants a big 'meat and
two veg' meal because he never gets to eat anything
but snacks during the day. So, um, oh, by the time I
get to think about what I want, I've lost interest!

Well, there's, like, my mum, my brother, and me and,
like, we almost never eat together especially during
the week. I mean, I get home from school around
4.30 or 5.00 and I'm always starving because school
food is so rubbish, so I just, like, grab some toast or
biscuits or something. Then my brother gets in
around 5.30 'cos he goes to a different school and
he's always in a rush to go out and play football, or
see his mates, or whatever. So, by the time mum gets
in from work, we've both kind of lost interest in food
so whatever she makes, and she's, like, a pretty good
cook, whatever it is we end up kind of picking at it in
front of the telly or my brother has it later when he
gets in. I kind of feel sorry for my mum; that she
always makes us something because she feels she
should but, um, to be honest I'm not that bothered
about food, sitting round the table and all that.

'Cos my mum gets in late, I sometimes, like, make my
brother something to eat if we're in at the same time
and once I remember I spent ages making a really
nice lasagne, all with, like, the proper vegetables and
sauce and stuff and he just, like, looked at it and sort
of spread it around his plate and that, and then just,
like, refused to eat it. And I mean, I felt just like my
mum must feel and I kind of yelled at my brother and
made a big fuss and chucked it all in the bin.

04 SO WHAT IS IT YOU DO?

Mark   So what do you do for a living Russell?
Russell I'm a fashion photographer.
Mark   Oh, right. So, um, does that mean you take
         pictures of models all over the world?
Russell Actually, yes it does, yes. I um, I, I take
         fashion and advertising images and I also

	direct, er, so I, I work within the mediums of film and photography.
Mark	Wow! So how long have you been doing that?
Russell	About, er, I would say about ten years in total ...
Mark	So what brings you to England right now?
Russell	I'm er, here meeting with a chap on, on, er, involved with the funding and, er, production of a film that I'm working on ...

| Russell | So what is it that you do, Mark? |
| Mark | Well, I've got two jobs. One is Management Training, and the other is composing music for film and TV. (Uhuh) Um, it's a little bit of a juggling act at the moment, because I'm not making enough from my music career, and I have to keep some funds coming in, so I do Management Training ...
I work with all kinds of household name businesses over here and I usually work with small groups of managers in the area of improving communication, er, communications, inter-relations, er, team-building, problem-solving, that type of area, um, and I've been doing that for about twenty years or so. But I've always been musical, and I've been a performer in the past, and, um, about seven or eight years ago I started composing ... and, um, I've done bits for the BBC, I did a wildlife series a few months ago (Uhuh) ... er, I've done bits for um, I've done a, an art piece, done music, a ten-minute piece for an art film. |

1
A What do you do for a living, then?
B I'm an Editor, um, I work for a TV listings magazine, you know the ones that tell you what's on what channel and when.

2
A What have you been up to work-wise?
B Well, actually, not that much. I went on a trip to the States a couple of months ago but since then it's all been rather quiet.

3
A So, er, how long have you been doing that, then?
B Ever since I left university really. I started off working in the box office and then gradually worked my way up.

4
A How's the job going?
B Er, fine, but, er, it's all a bit stressful at the moment, you know, what with the merger and all the staff changes.

5
A How did you get into that, then?
B Well, by accident really. I had an uncle who worked in the business, and one summer I went to work there just to get some experience of working in an office and it just went from there.

[icon] 4
A So what year are you in now?
B Year twelve.
A And what subjects are you doing?
B English literature, economics, and religious studies.
A And, how are you enjoying that?
B Yep. I like it. They're all very interesting.
A And, er, what are you planning to do after you leave school, do you know?
B I want to take a gap year and travel a bit and then maybe go to university afterwards, but I'm still not sure.

05 LOVE AT FIRST SIGHT

1 You're looking smart today!
2 I like your jacket. It really suits you.
3 Wow! You look absolutely stunning!
4 Mmm, nice perfume.
5 This is really delicious. You're such a good cook.
6 What lovely flowers!
7 Wasn't that a great party!
8 You're so good at organizing things.

06 HERE IS THE NEWS
[icon] 1

A

1 Reports are coming in of an earthquake in an outer suburb of San Francisco. The quake, measuring 7.2 on the Richter Scale, struck at 3.00 a.m. local time. Although the exact number of casualties has not been officially confirmed, it is feared that at least thirty-five people may have been killed, and the death toll is likely to rise. Hundreds more may have been left homeless or injured. Meanwhile, the suburb has been declared a disaster area, and rescue workers with sniffer dogs are being flown to the scene in a desperate race against the clock to rescue people trapped under the rubble.

2 The government has announced a crackdown on the publication of pornographic and racist literature on the Internet. A package of measures has been unveiled, which include imposing fines on Internet providers who authorize web sites containing material considered offensive, or unsuitable for children. Opposition politicians have attacked the plan, claiming that the measures would be too difficult to enforce. The proposals have also come under fire from civil liberties groups, who say that freedom of expression is a basic human right, and that individual governments should not be allowed to censor material published on the Internet.

3 There is grave concern in Birmingham over speculation that the city's largest car plant may be sold off to an unnamed multi-national company. Unions have warned that the sell-off could lead to the loss of thousands of jobs, and are due to meet the management of the company later today for urgent talks on the company's future.

4 There have been violent scenes in central London as police clashed with demonstrators who had gathered outside the Houses of Parliament to protest against the abolition of student grants. Police say that four people were detained for alleged criminal damage, and a further ten for criminal trespass. The organizers of today's rally say the aim was to hold a peaceful demonstration, and blamed the violence on a minority of people not involved with the student organizations.

B

1 The Foreign Secretary, Andrew Gardener, has resigned from the cabinet following allegations about his private life. Mr Gardener is understood to have handed in his resignation in a meeting with the Prime Minister earlier today. The allegations, which have been widely reported in the press, centre on an alleged relationship with an eighteen-year-old nightclub dancer. Mr Gardener, who is married with four children, has refused to comment on the rumours, insisting that he was standing down because he did not wish to cause any further embarrassment to the government or to his family. The Prime Minister has praised Mr Gardener, saying that he had been an outstanding Foreign Secretary. He will continue to represent his constituency as a Member of Parliament.

2 The Minister for Overseas Aid, Ms Rosemary Long, is to meet her European counterparts in Brussels tomorrow to discuss a package of measures aimed at cancelling debts owed by the world's poorest countries. Ms Long has insisted that stringent criteria must be met by developing countries before their debts could be written off. These include the establishment of democratic forms of government, and guarantees that any future aid donated by developed countries would be channelled to those most in need, and not into the pockets of corrupt leaders.

3 The supermarket chain, BLC, has announced that it's to eliminate GM ingredients from its own brand products from next April. Other supermarkets and food producers are likely to follow suit. The move follows customer pressure to ban foods made from genetically modified crops, replacing them with GM-free alternatives. According to the supermarket, the biggest problem facing them will be the eradication of genetically modified soya, since up to 60% of processed foods contain soya, most of it from the United States.

4 Scottish authorities have given assurances that there is no risk to the public after a reported breakdown in a nuclear power station near Strathclyde last night. Officials at the plant say there was a minor malfunction in the central operating system of the plant. They told reporters that there had been no leak of radioactivity, and that there is no cause for alarm.

[icon] 2

1 New research suggests that drinking coffee may increase the risk of heart disease and strokes. Scientists at Sussex University have found that both filtered and unfiltered coffee can pose a risk to health, and not simply unfiltered coffee, as had previously been believed.

2 A pet cat has survived after going through a complete washing cycle in an automatic washing machine. The cat's owner had said he didn't realize that the cat was in the machine when he loaded it up before going to work. The cat is reported to be dazed but unharmed. According to its owner, it is now making a full recovery, and is cleaner than ever before.

3 Passengers on a flight from Gatwick to the Isle of Wight were delayed for almost three quarters of an hour, when the plane had to circle the airport. Later, officials apologized to passengers, saying that the delay had been caused because the air traffic controller was out to lunch at the time.

4 Armed robbers who broke into a designer footwear shop in Manchester last night got away with a haul of boxes containing only left shoes. The owner of the shop explained that the right shoes were out on display at the time.

5 The Bank of England will announce later today whether it's to increase interest rates, which are currently at five and a quarter per cent. Unions have warned that an increase could threaten manufacturing jobs and further damage the economy.

1

A Have you heard the news about Ian and Linda?

B No, what's happened?

A Apparently they're going to split up.

B Oh no! Oh, what a shame! And they seemed so happy together.

A Yes, well apparently …

2

A Hey, guess what! I've just been invited to spend a week with Terry on his yacht in the Bahamas!

B Oh wow, lucky you! All right for some! When are you going?

3

A Are you OK?

B No, I've just had some bad news actually.

A What's the matter?

B I've just been given the sack.

A Oh no! Poor you! What happened?

4

A Dave was telling me that Alex has finally got her PhD.

B Oh wow! Good for her! When did she find out?

5

A Have you heard, there's supposed to be a rail strike tomorrow.

B Typical. Just when I have to get to Edinburgh …

6

A Hey, you'll never guess what I've just heard.

B What?

A Lynne's going to meet the Prime Minister.

B She isn't, is she? When?

7

A They were saying on the news that scientists have picked up signals from Mars.

B You're joking!

A Yes, it's true. Apparently they think there may be some form of life there.

07 HAVEN'T A CLUE

1

A Hi Paul, have you any idea where Ann is?

B Er, Ann, um … I'm not absolutely sure, but I've a feeling she may have popped out for a sandwich.

A Oh right. Any idea when she'll be back?

B Well, she's got an appointment at 2.00, so she should be back by then.

A OK, thanks.

2

A Jane, you don't happen to know Amy's e-mail address, do you?

B Not offhand, I'm afraid. Tim might know.

A No, he doesn't, I've already tried him.

B Have you tried asking Personnel? They ought to know.

A Oh, that's a good idea. I'll give them a ring.

3

A Excuse me, could you tell me if this is the right platform for the London train?

B No love, you want number five.

A OK, thanks very much.

B You're welcome, love.

4

A Excuse me, do you know if there's a vegetarian restaurant round here?

B Oh, er, let me see. Er, yeah, as far as I remember, there's one on, er, Broad Street, next to Marks and Spencer's.

A Sorry, I don't suppose you know if they serve vegan food too?

B Er, no, sorry, no idea, I'm afraid.

A Right, thanks anyway.

5

A Excuse me, I wonder if you could help me. I'm looking for Hayfield Road.

B Er, sorry, I'm a stranger here myself.

A Oh, er, OK, thanks.

6

A Hello, North-West Rail, how may I help you?

B Oh, um, hello. Erm, I'm ringing to enquire about times of trains to Manchester.

A Er, when are you travelling?

B Erm, I want to travel on Friday at around 5 o'clock …

7

A Yes?

B Oh, hello, I wonder if you could help me. I'm looking for information about car hire.

A Sorry, we don't actually keep details of car hire. You'll have to ask at the car hire desk. But I'm afraid it's shut at the moment.

B Oh no. Do you know what time it opens?

A Sorry, couldn't tell you, I'm afraid.

8

A Hello, Downside City Council.

B Hello, I'd like to speak to someone about rubbish collection.

A Hold the line please, I'll put you through to Environmental Services.

08 FARAWAY PLACES

A Mm. Windamere Hotel. I like the sound of this one.

B Oh yeah, what's it like, then?

A Er, it says here, 'The most refined and popular place to stay in Darjeeling, the Windamere is the perfect spot if you are looking for a little old world style and relaxation.'

B Oh, that sounds good.

A And lis…, listen to this, um, 'Open fires lit each night … er, blah blah blah blah … afternoon tea served on the lawn.' (Mm) I rather fancy open fires in the bedroom.

B And I like the sound of afternoon tea on the lawn. That's very civilized. What are the rooms like?

A Er, er, it says here, ah, 'bedrooms are basically furnished, with private shower (cold water only) and WC.'

B Hm, I wonder what they mean by 'basically furnished'.

A Mm. I don't, I don't really fancy the idea of cold showers.

B Yeah, sounds a bit too spartan for my liking.

A Still, the idea of an 'old colonial mansion' is quite appealing, I must say.

B Um, how much does it cost?

A Er, it doesn't say. You have to send away for a price list, I suppose.

B Well, maybe we should e-mail them and find out the prices.

A Yeah, yeah, let's do that.

09 CAUSE FOR CONCERN

A Who comes here, and what, what sort of, er, offences have they committed?

B Er, young men are sent here by courts who have committed really the full range of offences below murder or, although we have had actually people here for manslaughter, um, so the, the most common offences are robbery and burglary. Car crime, car thefts as well, er, dishonesty. We don't have any sex offenders here, there are other places that take sex offenders. But it's mostly offences of dishonesty and violence.

A Right, um, what do you think causes them to turn to crime?

B Well, as usual, we would have to say a full range of problems. Erm, you could list the following factors as one or more of them being present in all young men. One is family breakdown, er, where there's been divorce or breakdown between parents and um … because most of the young men here we find have been brought up either by one parent or by two parents who've had a very, um, poor relationship and they've not provided the proper care and love for that child. So it's, there are family problems behind first.

Um secondly, is poor housing and poor social conditions and poverty which they're in. Um, thirdly, um, is, um, unemployment, an un…, an inability to get work, for a lot of these young men, they, um, get excluded from school, there's a whole pattern, a common pattern where people, um, even the bright ones, might get excluded from school because of misbehaviour, or because they can't learn, they may be dyslexic, they may have problems with learning, they get excluded from school, hang around with other kids at risk, um, then start taking illegal drugs in a lot of cases, um, or they take alcohol too young and that goes to their head.

Approximately a third of young men here, for example, are here for crimes to feed a drug habit. So, either heroin or crack, um, especially for the over-eighteens, less so for the under-eighteens. But certainly that's in line with police figures from outside. So it's a combination of family and social problems, um, unemployment, er, drug abuse, er, inability to control, er, … figures have shown also a high number of kids have been abused, er, either sexually or violent abuse from parents, usually from a father. Um, lack of consistent good fathers is a key feature of the lives of most of these young men.

A Right, um, they mentioned things like, um, money. (Yep) How important do you think that is, wanting to live the high life, and …?

B Wanting to live the high life, there's tremendous peer group pressures, er, er, you know the, um, you know, trainers, all the flash gear, these cost a lot of money, the pressures to conform, to show that you can, er, live this high life, are very great on young people, and getting, er, that money legitimately when you've emerged from school even if you've stayed on at school with the right qualifications to get decent employment, to give a regular legal income is very hard, so the temptation to cut a corner is very very acute.

1

A … I'm in here because, um, I done a armed robbery and it was for the money … it was the money, simply the money, that's it. I was broke, so I had to go out there, do you get me?

B I'm in here for supplying heroin (Uhuh). I wanted to make money and live a good life. That's why I basically done it. There's a lot of money involved.

C I'm here for robbery and possession, just for earning some money, man …

2

A …I've had a lot of opportunities in prison, of getting myself out of there, to college, and getting qualifications, and I thought to myself, while I'm here, I might as well use up my time, so I was just sitting in my cell and … I think it's done me the world of good, basically.

B … I've gone to college, yeah, but I can't really concentrate because I'm in prison, so I'm not really learning nothing, basically. 'Cos when I come back and I try to do homework, can't do it, ... play something ... you know how it is, it's hard you see, so I'll have to really wait till I get out 'cos you can't really concentrate.

3

A Another thing, can I say something? (Yeah) You know this prison, like, I'm not saying this prison, prison actually, like, any prison, is a university of crime. You come in knowing about one crime, true, yeah?

B Yeah, true.

A You come in knowing about one crime, and you go out knowing about ten.

B True, true.

A 'Cos you're mixing with criminals, yeah, every day, 'Oh, do you know how to do this', yeah? Easy.

B You come in here, say you come here for a robbery or something ... and then you're on your way out, you might be thinking, I'll go straight or something, then, there's because there's so many people with different crimes, you might think 'Oh, I might be able to do that, I might be able to do that.' It's crazy, man.

A It is, it is. That's the skills you learn in prison.

B I thought I knew it all, yeah, but when I come in jail, I don't know nothing.

4

A Yeah, but you've got, like, different kinds of work, do you get me? You've got work that don't pay you nothing, and the work that they're going to try and give us, like, when we get out, yeah, we're not really qualified, yeah, so, when we get out we're gonna have to do them stupid jobs, yeah, and you don't make the money that we could be doing on crime.

B 'Cos when we get out of here we're going to have a criminal record, so, basically, we're at the back of the queue ... Like, who wants to employ an ex-criminal? Would you? That's how it is, that's how it is, (Yeah) so, like, we suffer, like, every way. We've come into prison, our families suffer, we suffer. We go out of prison, can't get a job.

5

B You can have ...

A It's fashion, innit? It's not fashion for ... to get the money, but, the styles that we're popping, and what we want to be driving, that's money, you get me, you've got to pay a lot of money for that stuff ...

B Well it was important, very important to me before, but now I think back, it was before, 'cos I needed to live a good life, so nice car, but now I think that it's not that important.

D What's made you change your mind, do you think?

B Family. Family's more important than anything. No money can buy that, no money ... Serious. That's what I've learned in prison. (Yeah)(That's true) Blood weighs more than money. To me that's true ... Yeah, I don't know ...

C It's true, it's true.

A What do you think is the best option for, um, rehabilitating young offenders?

B The best option is certainly not to bring them into custody, because they learn too many, um, tricks. They learn, it's, that in, in, some ways, however good a liberal prison, they still, the... they still, they are contaminated. So people who come here we find as first offenders, they will learn things that they wouldn't have learned outside. They get exposed, it is a very negative environment. So, um, I think that what has been proved to work is, outside, um, a lot of these young men have terrible problems of self-control, of thinking through choices, of thinking how to get the best out of situations, rather than, um, follow their impulses.

What has worked and been proved to work are what are called cognitive behaviour programmes with some of them, that despite all the factors I have mentioned, we, there are some offending behaviour programmes that do work, that do tackle people's, um, compulsiveness to offend, compulsiveness to take decisions before they think, um, not to think of the consequences. And programmes also that address their lack of employment skills. If people are given, um, qualifications, if they can emerge from, er, any college or prison or anywhere with qualifications that equip them for the job market, that means, in a lot of cases, basic education.

It has been proved that, um, something like ninety percent, for example, of the young prison population, because of their lack of basic education, are not equipped to even apply for ninety percent, about ninety percent, of the jobs available to them. So there's a huge educational programme needed. (Hm. Hm.) And it all proves that the two factors that, er, make a difference to people's chances when they come out of a prison sentence for example, is, one, getting into work. Employment is the key indicator. And secondly, having a strong family support, some kind of, whether it's a partner or a parent, some constructive help outside. Those two factors are the key indicators, research have shown. Without realistic chances of employment, and getting into work, and without family support, um, people, the temptation to drift back into crime is overwhelming.

10 WHERE WAS I?

Lynne Anyway, as I was saying, I went to this really interesting seminar the other day, (Oh yeah) about cross-cultural awareness.

Colin Oh, hang on, that's, that's the one with the Romanian woman?

Lynne Yes, up at the university. (Uhuh) And it was really strange, because she was saying that even the most normal thing can be quite different in different societies.

Colin What do you mean?

Lynne Well, for example, the guy behind us who was married to a Hungarian woman, he was saying that whenever his wife rang up his family, her family, er, whenever they were talking, if someone was talking for a long time, they never interrupted each other, never said (What?)'Yes', 'No', 'Really', 'Oh, I see', and things like that.

Colin What did they say?

Lynne Nothing.

Colin Nothing at all?

Lynne Absolutely nothing. Erm, because if you do, if you say all these sorts of things that we normally say, then you find that the person thinks you're rude, and they think you're trying to stop them and to interrupt them, and it's really annoying.

Colin You know what, that reminds me of, of France actually, because when I (Really?) first went to France, you know how in England if you ask for a light, (Yeah) you know, if you're a smoker like me, and you ask someone in the street for a light (Yeah) you go up and you say, 'Well, excuse me have you got a light?', 'Yes, certainly, here you are', (Uhum) 'Thanks very much', 'You're welcome', 'Bye'. You know, there's a whole conversation around it, but in France it's not like that at all. (Isn't it?) You just go up, and you say 'Have you got a light?' (Uhuh) and they don't say anything at all just (Nothing at all?), there it is, and that's it, you know, and that's really disconcerting (It is a bit) if you're used to all the, all the chat and ...

Lynne Yes, uhuh, I mean I find something like that quite, quite difficult to get used to (Yeah) because we're so very different (Mm) Anyway, what I was, where was I? What I was going to say was, one of the things she tried to get at, one of the points she was trying to make was that we need to think about how we show respect, and to do that we need to ...

12 HOW WE MET

Hanne So, how, how did you meet David?

Jane Well, I was going shopping one day, I'd been living in East Oxford for about five years, (Yeah) with my two boys, and I'd been having a boring sort of weekend doing some painting (Yeah) and, and I thought, 'Well, it's time to go out and stock up on some things.' Tom was about to have his eighth birthday, (Oh right) so I was getting some birthday stuff (Yeah) um, so I set off to the supermarket. And then I was trundling around Sainsbury's with my trolley, when suddenly, um, this rather interesting-looking man appeared at the ice cream counter (Oh no) yeah, and he ...

Hanne What, shopping as well, or working there?

Jane No, I think, well, yeah, he was definitely shopping. (OK) He'd got a trolley (Right) and he sort of hung around a bit and helped himself to some ice cream and, um, talked to me about what sort of ice cream I wanted, and why was I buying it.

Hanne What, he just, he just started talking to you?

Jane Yeah, amazingly friendly, I thought (Mm, yeah). Um ... And we established that I was having a party for my son, and that he'd got a son as well, and, um, then off I went and did some more shopping and filled up my trolley, and then when I got to the checkout ...

Hanne And he went another way?

Jane Yeah, (Yeah) and there he was again, um, right behind me (Oh) and we had a chance to do a little bit more talking and found out that he'd got three sons and I'd got two sons (Right) and I checked out his finger and, to see if he was married, and he didn't seem to be and nor was I, and so this was getting quite interesting (Right, yeah) but then of course it was time for me to pay, (Mm) so I packed up all my, my shopping and went towards the door thinking, 'Oh, that's a shame, I'm never going to see him again', (Yeah, exactly) and then I suddenly realized I was going to see him again because I hadn't paid, so I had to ...

Hanne Oh no, (I know) what, because you were talking to him and you'd just walked off?

Jane I know, yes, not the sort of thing I usually do. So I had to come back and quickly get out my cheque book, and I was very embarrassed because I ...

Hanne And was he still there?

Jane Yeah, (Oh no) and I thought, 'Oh, he's going to think she's really a criminal not paying for her, her shopping.' So I, I paid eventually, and, and (Right) went away and thought, 'Oh, what a shame, I go to parties and meet (Yeah, exactly) extremely boring men and here's an interesting-looking guy in Sainsbury's, and I'll never see him again.' So I went home, (Mm), did a bit of painting, and decided I wouldn't think anything more about it (Yeah) and then about eight o'clock that night he telephoned. (No) Yeah.

Hanne The Sainsbury's guy?
Jane Yeah. And it was amazing because I wasn't, I'd only just moved house so I wasn't in the directory and what he'd done (Yeah, how had he done it?) he'd, he'd found out my name by looking at my cheque book when I (Right), when I wrote my cheque (Oh God, clever) and then, um, rung Directory Enquiries, found out new numbers, tried, tried a few, a few numbers before he discovered that and finally ...
Hanne So he tried completely wrong numbers?
Jane Yeah, asking for Jane Bingham and being told off by fierce fathers and things. And then finally he got through to me and asked if I'd be very brave and go out to dinner with him.
Hanne Oh, that's so romantic.
Jane I know. So, um, I did go out to dinner with him and I was a bit nervous because you're not really meant to go on dates with people you've picked up in supermarkets. And I told a few friends I was, what I was doing. And then he turned up with a great big bunch of flowers, and I could tell it was all going to be all right.
Hanne And it was all right?
Jane It was fine.
Hanne Oh, that's fantastic.

[◦ 2]

Hanne And talking about romantic stories, I've, I've got one too, but it's, it's not about me, it's about a friend of mine (Mm) who, um, was working out in the Algarve with me in, in Portugal. And I think I told you, when I was there we used to all go out in plane loads (Yeah) and I was one plane load in front of her and she, she was sitting at the airport and she'd been, she'd had a few drinks and she was feeling quite depressed 'cos she'd sort of had quite a bad time man-wise recently, and a lot of people had let her down, and she was just feeling a bit down in the dumps. (Yeah) You know she was, I think she was thinking, 'Right, this is it, I'll go to Portugal and I'll leave it all behind.' Anyway, she went to check in, to get on the flight and everything, and she went through the second part of the check-in and there was this pretty nice man sort of (Mm) doing the passports and doing the tickets, and er, she looked at him and she thought, 'Ooh, well you're, you're really attractive, I think you're great', and they had this eye contact moment but, but nothing else really (Yeah) and then she passed on and sort of thought 'Well, that was nice, but that was it.' Anyway, she flew out to Faro, landed, came through the passport check-out thing again, picked up her luggage, came into the arrivals hall, and there he was. (You're joking.) No, there he was, the man from Heathrow.
Jane How did he get there?
Hanne Well, he, apparently he'd, I don't know how it worked logistically but he'd got on another plane, 'cos there were lots of them

going that day for the season, and he'd managed to get there first. And 'cos obviously he can just, he's, he's an official at the airport, he could just run straight through. And the best thing was that he'd gone and collected all the sort of welcome flowers (Yeah) that all the health clubs give you (Yeah) and he'd got them all in a great big bouquet and there he was, the doors sort of parted and there he was with this great big bunch of flowers and (Amazing) they're married as well now, but living in Portugal.
Jane Really romantic. Fantastic.

[◦ 6]

Have, have I told you about the time I was trekking in the Andes? ... Well, yeah, it was about six years ago ... and, um, I was climbing up through the mountains, and aiming to stay overnight in a base camp ... a base camp is one of those places where the mountaineers stay before they attempt the summit of a mountain ... Anyway, I'd been trekking all day ... I was quite tired, it was getting late, quite dark, quite cold ... I got to the top of the mountain, and I didn't have a tent with me because I'd read in my guidebook that, um, there are huts where you can stay when you get to the top, mountaineering huts ... and sure enough, there were several little huts ... um but they were all full of mountaineers ... and I went round knocking on all of the doors saying, 'Look, um, I've come here without a tent, can I stay in your hut please?' ... and they all said 'No, no, I'm afraid it's full.' ... So I went away and I thought, 'What am I going to do? Am I going to just sleep out in the open and freeze, or am I going to try again?'... So I decided to try again and I knocked on um, one hut and I said 'Look, please can I share your hut with you?' ... and they said 'No, I'm sorry, the hut is full ... but, um, we do have a spare tent, and if you like, you can stay out in our spare tent.' ... So fortunately I was able to sleep in the tent, um, and I was OK, but it taught me one thing, and that is, don't believe what you read in guidebooks.

13 HOW CAN I PUT THIS?

[◦ 1]

1
A Hey, who's been at my chocolates?
B Not me.
A Oh, come on, I bet you have. There was five here this morning. There's only one left.
B Well, OK, I, I did take one.
A Oh, it doesn't matter.
B It was really nice.
A It's OK.

2
A You know we arranged to play squash this evening?
B Oh, you're not going to say you can't come, are you?
A Well, the thing is, I've got so much work to do that I'm going to have to stay here till about eight o'clock.
B Oh, never mind. How about another night?
A Yeah, well, shall we try Thursday? That might be better.
B OK.

3
A Um, you know that Beethoven CD you lent me?
B My favourite one?
A Yeah, um, I'm afraid it's got a bit scratched.
B Oh no, you're joking.
A Well, I ... unless it was already like that? Um, I'm, I'm really sorry.
B I'm sure it wasn't like that. Oh well, don't worry.

A I, I'll get you another one.
B Thank you.

4
A Anna, um, have you got a moment?
B Um, yes, yes, fine. What did you want?
A The thing is, um, we have to reach this deadline on Friday, and we're running very close. Would you mind working overtime this evening and tomorrow? A couple of hours extra?
B Um, I'll have to phone home first, but that should be OK.
A That's great.

5
A Hi, Oonagh. How are you?
B Fine. How are you?
A Very well, thank you. Um, I've got a couple of tickets for the opera. I wondered if you'd like to come along?
B To the opera? Um, that's really kind of you, but, to be honest, I'm not very keen on the opera.
A Oh, OK. Oh well, never mind.

6
A Gerry?
B Yeah?
A Um, I've got a bit of a problem. The thing is, my babysitter's just cancelled and I really need somebody for tonight. Could you see your way to doing it for me?
B Well, I, Greg, I'd love to help you out but I'm afraid my car's broken, I can't, I can't get there.
A Oh dear, that's a shame. Thanks anyway.
B OK.

7
A Oh, Melinda, (Yeah) do you want a hand with the washing up?
B No, it's OK, thanks, I can manage this myself.

8
A I'm going home your way today. Would you like a lift?
B Oh, would that be all right? Wouldn't be too much trouble?
A No, that'be fine. There's plenty of room in the car.
B Erm, yeah, that'be great. I haven't got any money for a taxi, so fantastic.

[◦ 2]

1
A Could I ask you a big favour?
B Sure, what's the matter?
A Well the thing is, my neighbour was going to feed my cat while I was away on holiday but unfortunately she had to go away herself. I don't suppose there's any way you could feed the cat for me, is there?

2
A You know I said I could lend you my car this weekend ...?
B Yeah, is there a problem?
A Well, yeah, you could say that. You'll never believe what happened last night ... I was just pulling away from the traffic lights when this idiot crashed right into the side of my car. He'd obviously shot straight through a red light.

3
A Have you got a moment?
B Um, sure, what's the problem?
A Do you think you could explain how I can copy this document into this folder? I've been trying for ages but I can't seem to do it.

4
A I've got a bit of a problem ...
B Oh dear, what's happened?
A I've got a friend from Italy coming to stay at the weekend but the ceiling in the spare room has collapsed.

B Oh no, what a nightmare!
A I don't suppose she could sleep at your place, could she? She's very nice, you know ...

5
A You know that book you lent me ...?
B Yeah ...?
A Well, I'm really sorry but I was reading it in the bath and I dropped it in the water ... it's OK but the pages are a bit curly!

6
A I don't quite know how to put this, but you know ...
B What's the matter?
A Well, it's about the holiday. I know I said you could come along with us, but the thing is, Jake's already invited his girlfriend and I don't see how we're all going to fit in the car.

7
A Er, there's something I've been meaning to tell you ...
B What, what's the matter?
A Well, you know John and I have been seeing quite a lot of each other lately?
B Yeah ...?
A Well, the thing is, we're a bit more than just friends now.

8
A I'm afraid I've got an apology to make.
B Oh?
A I'm afraid I've accidentally spilt coffee on your carpet. I'm really sorry.

14 WE'VE BEEN HAD

Part 1
Newsreader
And finally, the story of Edwin Sabillon, the little boy whose epic journey from Honduras to New York and his quest to find his father won the hearts of the nation. It turns out that Edwin was telling a tall tale. When police efforts to trace his father failed, and news of his plight hit the national headlines, police discovered that the only part of Edwin's story with any grounding in reality was his journey from Miami, where he had been living with his Aunt Aurora for several years. The rest, it seems, was the product of an over-active imagination and the age-long desire to strike it rich on the streets of New York. Officer Granger from the New York Police sums up the reaction of the force at having been taken in by the ten-year-old.

Officer Granger
Well, what can I say? We've been had. Some people might say this makes us look kind of dumb, but I guess you could say it shows we're not just hard nosed cops. We have this reputation of being tough, of being hard-hearted, street-wise, and all the rest, but we try to help folks when they're in trouble, we have a heart the same as anyone else does. So I guess there's a silver lining for us there.

Part 2
Newsreader
On the streets of downtown Manhattan, reactions were mixed.

A
I think it's a shame. I honestly believed he made that journey, I felt sorry for the kid, you know, he was an orphan, he was down on his luck. I guess I feel kinda let down.

B
I feel disappointed, to be honest with you. It seems like you can't take anyone at their word nowadays. Everyone's just out for what they can get, they trick people, they tell lies, and everyone thinks, wow, that

sure is smart. He made up all those terrible things about his family, and now he's going to get away with it. And not just get away with it, he's gonna be some kind of big celebrity. I think that sucks. We've got all our values upside down, if you ask me.

C
I believed him. I genuinely believed him. Now he's made everyone look stupid, you know what I'm saying? And the cops? They've really got egg on their faces.

D
I'm glad for the kid. I'm glad people have reached out to him, like, offered him money, offered him clothes, sent him roller blades, all that stuff, like they said on the news. People in New York have really taken him to their hearts. I'm proud we're such a fine bunch of people.

E
I say good luck to him. He's an enterprising kid, he fooled the New York Police. Jeez, he took us all for a ride. With an acting talent like he has, he deserves to do well. Maybe he'll go on to win an Oscar, maybe he'll write a best-selling novel, hey, who knows? He's got a good future ahead of him, that's for sure.

Newsreader
And it seems that Edwin's future is indeed now secured. The New York Police Department have been flooded with offers to adopt him, including one from the taxi-driver who rescued him, Edward Basora. And as for the NYPD, the whole episode has revealed a human side that is not usually on display.

A I knew a guy who lied every day.
B What, you mean he was a compulsive liar?
A Well, he felt he had to lie, because he was so embarrassed about losing his job, and, er ...
B Hang, hang on, how did he lose his job?
A Well, he had a disagreement over a, a pay rise. (Right) It was in Japan, and it was very shameful to, er, have lost your job, and he couldn't face, um, telling his wife's family that, er ... that he was without a job ...
B What, so his wife was Japanese?
A Yes, his wife was Japanese, yeah. And, um, he went out of the house every day at the same time as if he was going to work, carrying his briefcase, and came back at the same time.
B So, so, hang on, what was he doing then, if he was going out?
A He was just looking for work and, er, going to interviews and talking to people trying to find a job, sitting in cafés. And he wouldn't be able to come home until he would normally come home at the end of his working day.
B So what happened in the end then, did he find a job?
A He found a job, and, er, his behaviour didn't change he just kept going out to work at the same time.

15 BEHIND THE WHEEL

A
Ladies and gentlemen, the motion we are debating this evening is, do cars do more harm than good? And clearly, the answer is yes, on a number of counts. First and foremost, cars are responsible for the deaths of 100,000 people a year, and leave over 50,000 people seriously injured. Secondly, on pollution grounds alone, the car poses a major threat to our planet and our health. Exhaust emissions from motor vehicles are hastening the deaths of up to 24,000 people each year, and indeed forcing many other people with respiratory ailments, such as asthma, to

stay indoors for large parts of the year. We can no longer open our windows, and instead have to use air conditioning; and as we know, CFCs from air conditioning are a major cause of climate change. And then there's the issue of congestion. Cars not only clog up the streets and make life unpleasant for shoppers, tourists, and pedestrians, but they are even failing to transport us quickly to where we want to go. Rush hour traffic jams cause thousands of motorists to arrive at their workplaces late and in a state of advanced stress, and at their worst can lead to road rage; and in Bangkok it's impossible to make more than one business appointment a day because you simply can't guarantee that you'll arrive on time. Cars also impose a financial burden in terms of health care; the thousands and thousands of pounds of taxpayers' money spent on treating people with respiratory ailments and the victims of car accidents; and in terms of congestion, which is costing the economy £15 billion every year in London alone. And finally, we need to think about the effect cars are having on our environment. There is no doubt that cars are starting to destroy our entire way of life. We are ripping out the heart of our historic cities to build more roads and ugly multi-storey car parks; and we are cutting through whole swathes of unspoilt countryside to create noisy pollution-producing motorways.

Because of cars, huge, out-of-town shopping centres have grown up that are killing the corner shop, taking the life out of our city centres, and we are making life increasingly difficult for the old, the poor, the elderly, the disabled, and indeed for anyone who's not a car-owner. In short, ladies and gentlemen, it seems to me that unless we restrict the use of cars, we are simply going to exacerbate the problem.

What we should be doing is using public transport and our legs more, and using our cars less; for the sake of our health, our culture, and indeed our planet. Thank you.

B
Ladies and gentlemen, it's quite frankly absurd to suggest that cars do more harm than good. Cars enhance people's lives, they're great liberators, and they give people choices. Now, people will argue that cars cause pollution. Of course, nobody wants pollution, nobody wants congestion, but it's simply not fair to put the blame on cars. Cars these days are getting much much cleaner, and much quieter and safer too, for that matter.

What is mainly responsible for pollution is the diesel engine. Diesel emissions actually contain forty of the most carcinogenic substances known to man, and as we all know, diesel engines are fitted in buses. As for congestion, well, no doubt you've all heard nightmare scenarios of gridlocked roads, traffic at a permanent standstill, but this could easily be solved by building more roads where they're needed. And it's simply not true to say that cars clog up city centres, because most of the day they're parked out of the way in car parks. It is misconceived policies by planners, and a shortage of roads, that are causing the problems, not cars.

And let's not forget the financial benefits cars bring to the country. The car industry provides some ten thousand jobs, not to mention the thirty odd million pounds in revenue from car tax, road tax, and tax on fuel. And finally, there's the issue of convenience. The fact is that public transport does not and cannot meet everyone's transport needs. People need to travel in and out of cities at different times and in different directions, and there are people living in the country who have no alternative but to use a car.

Quite frankly, I find it astonishing that the anti-car lobby should expect car-owners to spend thousands of pounds on buying their cars, taxing and insuring them, and then leave them at home and spend a small fortune on an inadequate public transport system that takes them nowhere near where they want to go. Ladies and gentlemen, let's live in the real world. The simple fact of the matter is, the car is here to stay. We like them, and we've got used to having them. You can't legislate to stop people using their cars. Ban them from the city centre and they'll simply go elsewhere. Instead of **declaring war on cars**, what we need to do is accommodate them and come up with creative ideas for making life easier for the motorist. Thank you.

16 WHAT ARE YOUR PLANS?

Conversation 1
A Have you got any plans for the weekend?
B Yeah, I think on Friday night I'm, I'm going em salsa dancing.
A Uhuh, to your usual place?
B Yes, I'll meet up with some friends, (Uhuh) I'm going to, yeah, probably stay up quite late.
A Uhuh, how late?
B Well, I don't know. Usually about 3.00. How about you, what are your, what are your plans?
A Um, I'm going up to Nottingham to visit some friends up there, and, er, I'm just going to stay the night, have a meal, and come back down the next day.
B So you're coming back on Saturday?
A Yes, yeah, yeah, 'cos (Yeah) I've got a party on Saturday night.
B Um, oh, (Yeah) very busy.

Conversation 2
A So, have you any plans for this weekend?
B Well, pretty much the same plans as every weekend, (Uhuh) I'll be playing cricket one day ...
A Really?
B Er, probably on Sunday. And, er ...
A If the weather lets you.
B How about you?
A Um, I'm going to have a lazy weekend. Um, I'm going to be packing, sorting out things, so that when I fly away next Wednesday, it won't be too much of a headache.

Conversation 3
A What are you doing at the weekend then, Katharine?
B Um, Friday night I'm just going out for a meal, and I'm going to see my parents. Um, Saturday, I'll probably go to the gym and just do things round the house, and then Saturday night I'm going ten-pin bowling, so quite an active weekend. I think Sunday I shall just crash out and do nothing.
A Yeah, catch up with everything.
B What are you doing?

Conversation 4
A Have you got anything exciting planned for the weekend, then?
B No, not really, I, I was going to go round to Naomi's but unfortunately she's got flu, so she's had to call it off.
A Oh no, what a shame.
B Um, yeah. I, I'd quite like to go on that trip to Bath though, but it depends on whether they've got any places left.

18 FROM ANOTHER PLANET?

Extract A
Jane So, you're, you're saying that you think far more of the person is, is genetic, and not influenced by their upbringing?
Nick Yes, I think so. I think, you look at twins, even identical twins, they have very different personalities, very different characteristics, or three children brought up in a family, er, the same environment, but radically different personalities, and, if I take an example from my own family, I have an elder sister who's very very ambitious, very very um career-orientated, er, very very determined, quite materialistic in fact.
Jane But you're, but you're just looking at one side of it, you're looking at it just from the genetic point of view. But no two people even in the same family have exactly the same experience. They don't have the same influences on them. The first child is treated incredibly differently from the second child. Twins are treated differently.
Nick I see what you're saying, but I still believe that, er, from my own experience, that um, in ..., inherited characteristics play a very very strong part in determining the character of the individual.
Jane Yeah, I was only talking in theory that, that ... I'm arguing that ... the whole balance seems to have swung to the importance of nature not nurture, and I think this pendulum has swung too far, and that it needs to come back to the point where, um, upbringing, conditioning, society, all the influences after the child is born, I think still as, they should be seen as more important than the genetic make-up.

Extract B
Nick So are you arguing that boys and girls should be treated in exactly the same way from the day that they're born? Is that what you're saying?
Jane I don't think it's possible because we're all products of our own upbringing. Boys and girls are treated so differently in a family, boys really, still, are not expected to cook or sew or even simple things like make their beds or do the washing up. (Mm) Whereas little girls are taught that this is playing, that if they learn to do this, and if they do it as a game, it's playing at being adult, (Mm) and, and they, they think it's great fun and they enjoy it, and they're they get conditioned into doing it and the boys get ... are conditioned to not do it. Why still does Granny knit something blue for a baby boy and something pink for a baby girl? It's so, it's so deep within our culture to treat boys and girls differently. Um, I mean, what do you think, do you think they should be treated much more similarly? Or allowed to develop in their own way and not stereotyped?
Nick Absolutely. I couldn't agree more. I think that parents should allow children to be who they really are, and who they want to be, regardless of their, er, sex. I do however think that inherently boys like cars and trains, not all boys ... by any means ...
Jane Oh, that's rubbish!
Nick It's not rubbish.
Jane It is rubbish.
Nick Oh, come on Jane!
Jane Boys inherently like cars and trains?

Nick Well let me take the example of a friend of mine who has two young children. And the boy loves *Thomas the Tank Engine*, has them in his room, and his sister can go in his room and play with any of his toys at any time that she wants, but she much prefers to stay in her room and play with her dolls and her make-up sets and her combs, and her brushes.
Jane But she's ...
Nick She has complete choice.
Jane She's trying to be different from him though. Of course you, I mean to some extent you admire your sister or your brother but you want to be different.

Extract C
Nick I think it's more a question of playing to your strengths. And as a boy you often realize that you're stronger than girls. Or men know that they're physically stronger than women ... but I think that's a very interesting point, because I think the scene is shifting in today's day and age. For example, I would always send my wife to the garage to get the car mended, because I know she can, can charm the male mechanics working at the garage, whereas if I took it in, I wouldn't be able to charm them in the same way. Just as, um, I will, I don't know, fix a shelf which is higher up because I'm physically taller than she is.
Jane But you're, you're saying that's genetic, it's genetic that the woman is better at getting round men in a garage and that genetically men are really good at putting up shelves.
Nick No, I'm not saying that, I think people adjust to their environment and evolve, if you look at Princess Diana for example, I mean she was incredibly clever, I mean she wasn't a stereotypical downtrodden woman, was she? I mean she came across as being much stronger, much more in control than Prince Charles, and stereotypically, or traditionally, it's the man who is strong and in control. I don't believe that's true. I think fundamentally women are stronger, more resourceful than men and I think men, because they're physically stronger and they're genetically, they've evolved to be physically stronger, believe that they have to play this role of being the provider or the carer, but I think it's, er, it's, er, an illusion in a lot of domestic relationships and that there's the strong role and the supporting role is played by the woman and not the men.

Extract D
Nick The point you're making is a good one, and I think if we look at men and women as they get older, and move into the workplace, I think women today are increasingly empowered in the workplace and we can see more and more women leading independent ...
Jane Oh, that's a tiny minority of women who are 'empowered'.
Nick But it's more and more, ... we can see more and more women moving into management positions in companies today, being ambitious in the way that men traditionally were ... and in some cases, you could cite Mrs Thatcher as an example, they want to be a very powerful, independent, ambitious, career-minded person.
Jane But they're not being themselves, they're just copying the only model that, that they've got.

19 ABSOLUTELY UNBELIEVEABLE!

A

Jerry I had the most embarrassing experience when I was on holiday, have I told you about this? I was in a bar in Spain.

Liz I don't think so, no.

Jerry Um right, there were two of us and, and I'd just had a glass of beer, we'd both just had a glass of beer and my glass was sitting empty on the table, and it was one of these marble-topped tables (Yeah, I know what you mean) and it was lunch time and this bar was full of people having their, having their lunch (Uhuh) um, and I must just have caught the edge of the glass with my finger and it fell over, it was like slow motion. It was one of those horrifying moments where everything slows down and you could see it just reach the point of balance and then fall, and it hit the table and completely exploded. It just went everywhere ... (What a nightmare!) It was absolutely unbelievable, I just felt like standing up and running out of the bar, and this glass sprayed out across the whole bar, and landed in everyone's lunch. And probably twelve or fifteen people just had, just couldn't eat any more and had to stop. It was unbelievable, (Oh, Jerry!) I've never been so embarrassed in my life.

Liz I can't believe that, that's the most embarrassing story I've ever heard.

B

Liz Have I told you about my Christmas holiday?

Jerry No, you haven't, no.

Liz I had the most extraordinary experience. I was, ended up going up the mountain on one of those sort of motorized sledge things, do you know what I mean, it's kind of, it's like a motorbike on two runners, (Oh yeah, yeah, I know the ones) you know what I mean. OK, we had to go, we had to use this thing to get up to the restaurant where we were going to have dinner, and I was on it with two other friends, um, one of my friends was driving it and ...

Jerry So there, sorry, there were three of you on this thing?

Liz Yeah, three of us, one driving and two sitting on the sledge attachment at the back, (right) and um, my friend at the front was driving incredibly fast up this mountain, it was freezing cold, pitch black, couldn't see a thing, um, and we suddenly got to this point, and there was a huge bump of snow in the middle of the piste, (Oh no) and so this snow-sledge thing went flying over the bump, I disappeared off the back of the sledge, at great speed, um, my other friend was left holding on. And my friend who was driving just carried on up the mountain ... (Oh no) she didn't realize I'd fallen off the back ...

Jerry So what happened, did she ... ?

Liz My, the second friend was screaming 'Stop, stop, stop the sledge, Liz has fallen off', but she couldn't hear 'cos it was so noisy. Anyway, eventually the friend driving realized and stopped, and they had to turn around and come and pick me up and I was covered in snow. Luckily I landed in a big soft bit.

Jerry Ah, but you were all right, were you?

Liz Yeah I was, I was fine.

Jerry Wow. That reminds me of a time when I was skiing in Switzerland, and we were coming down the hill ...

1

I was on my way home from this party, it must have been about 2.00 in the morning, and I was sure there was someone following me, so I was walking really fast. I got to my front door and I was just putting the key into the lock, when suddenly next door's cat leapt off the wall, practically into my face ...

I was absolutely petrified. It frightened the life out of me.

2

... and I came out of the hotel, put my bags in the car, and drove off. At least I thought I'd put my bags in the car but in fact I'd left one of them on the roof and there I was driving down the High Street with my bag on the roof, and these people shouting and beeping at me. I was wondering what on earth the problem was and was getting quite annoyed when I suddenly realized what I'd done ...

It was so embarrassing. I went bright red, removed it from the roof and drove off as quickly as I could.

3

This is a good one my Dad told me ... it was years ago, in the sixties I think, and he was on a long-haul flight to Delhi I think it was, and the last leg of the flight was with an Indian airline. And they came around with some food and stuff and when everyone had finished, they brought round these hot hand towels, you know the ones you sometimes get in restaurants, and my Dad really didn't know what this was for and he tried to take a bite out of it ... can you imagine!

It was absolutely awful. He nearly died of embarrassment.

4

... and I'd ordered this computer and printer, which they said they would deliver within ten days. And you won't believe what they did, the idiots, they left all this expensive equipment in my unlocked garage, and surprise, surprise, by the time I got home, it had all been stolen.

I was absolutely livid. I nearly hit the roof when I realized what had happened.

5

I'd already written about half my dissertation when my computer crashed and I lost all my files. And of course I hadn't backed any of them up on disk ...

It was an absolute nightmare. I just felt like bursting into tears.

6

I took my nephew to the zoo last Sunday and I'd just bought him an ice cream and so he was quite happy, eating away and looking at the giraffes over this fence. And anyway, all of a sudden, one giraffe put its neck over the fence and took a huge great bite of my nephew's ice cream.

It was absolutely hilarious. We were both in stitches.

20 A BIT OF PROBLEM

Conversation 1

Hello, you're through to Softbacks Unlimited. I'm afraid all our lines are busy at the moment. Please hold the line, and one of our sales assistants will be with you as soon as possible ...

A Good Morning, Softbacks Unlimited. This is Kerry speaking, how may I help you?

B Oh, um, hello, er, I'm phoning about a book I ordered from you.

A Right, if I could just take your name?

B Er, Gaynor Jones.

A And your customer number?

B Er, it's, um, 2040 5683.

A Right, Ms Jones, if you could just bear with me a few seconds ... Right, it's just coming up on the screen now. Won't be long ... OK, here it is, *The Rough Guide to New York*. Ordered on May 10th.

B Yes. The thing is, er, I need it rather urgently.

A Um, well, with respect, Ms Jones, we only received your order ten days ago. We promise to send books within three weeks of receiving your order.

B Yes, yes, of course, I, I do understand. The thing is, I, I'm going to New York in a week's time. I was rather hoping it would arrive by the end of the week. I don't suppose there's any way you could send it a bit earlier?

A Certainly, Ms Jones, that's no problem at all. I'll do my best to get that off to you straight away.

Conversation 2

A Hello, Benson Software. You're through to Customer Services.

B Hello, this is Mike Williams from Smiths Retailers of Portsmouth. I'm phoning about the CD-ROM consignment you sent last week. Um, I'm afraid there's a bit of a problem.

A Oh, right, Mr Williams.

B Er, I'm afraid you don't seem to have sent us enough.

A Oh dear. I'm sorry about that. How many did you receive?

B Well, we received fifty, but I'm pretty sure we ordered a hundred and fifty.

A Just a moment, I'll check your order ... Well, according to our records, you seem to have ordered fifty.

B Oh, really? Oh, perhaps there's been a mistake. I feel certain we ordered a hundred and fifty.

A OK, Mr Williams, sorry about the misunderstanding. We'll get the extra hundred to you as soon as possible.

B Thanks very much. Sorry to trouble you.

A No problem. Goodbye.

21 TALKING PICTURES

Pru So, Jon, what did you think of the film?

Jon Er, overall, er, it was mildly entertaining. Er, as a thriller, it didn't really have many thrills, er, but, um, on the other hand, it was, it had, it had merits, it was quite nice to look at. Er, the acting was pretty poor. What, what did you feel about it?

Pru I thought that Jude Law was good in it, but I agree with you that the rest of the acting was a bit poor. I thought Matt Damon didn't have any menace to his character at all, which made the story a bit unbelievable as a whole. (Yeah) Did you find the story believable?

Jon Absolutely unbelievable. Um, its, its premise was completely farcical, and I really didn't fall for it in any way whatsoever. Um, and like you I, I, I felt Matt Damon was weak, but, er, certainly not as weak as the, er, the supporting actors who were characteristically awful.

Pru But it was a beautiful film to look at, did you think?

Jon Absolutely. And myself, coming from a background where I know quite a lot about, er, the beautiful landscapes of Italy, I enjoyed watching it very much, um, but it can't, I can't help feeling that overall it, it's, it was just a question of style over substance.

Pru I found the ending quite shocking in the way that you didn't see the characters, you just heard them talking and knowing that a murder was going to take place. Did you find that quite, um, upsetting?

Jon No, really, no, I didn't enjoy the ending at all and, er, it, it didn't add anything to the story for me. Um, I felt it was rather inconclusive and I wish, I wish there had been something more exciting really at the end. But as it was it just felt like it was just petering out and it was just going to probably have another sequel which is what so many films do these days. Still, how many marks would you give it out of ten altogether?

Pru I'd probably give it seven out of ten.

Jon Seven? Six for me.

 2

Rob I saw a great film the other day, yeah ...

Conal Did you, what was it?

Rob *English Patient*. Have you seen that?

Conal Oh, yeah, I saw that, it was fantastic, wasn't it?

Rob Yeah, what did you think of it?

Conal Well, I'm I, I'm not sure I, I thought it was brilliant and it was better if you had read the, the book.

Rob Oh, right, yeah, OK, I've not read the book.

Conal There were parts of the, the characters that weren't filled in in the movie but were, were in the book.

Rob Right, OK. Well, I was, I was kind of a bit nervous when I went it see it 'cos I'd heard it was, um, a bit over-romantic, (Right) people had been telling me it was a bit ...

Conal It was a bit cl..., a bit of a classic wasn't it really?

Rob Yeah, that's right.

Conal Very, um, kind of traditional big picture kind of romance.

Rob But I don't think that was very bad, I mean, I don't think that was a bad thing particularly.

Conal Well, I think if you went in with certain expectations, (Yeah) er, you know, you have to suspend disbelief a little bit about it and the kind of great epic ending and things.

Rob Yeah.

Conal But I thought it was really, I thought it was quite moving and, er ...

Rob Yeah, and, very moving, I think a lot of the people in the cinema were crying at the end, I think that's a good sign.

Conal Yeah, what did you think of the cinematography and stuff like that?

Rob It's very impressive I mean er, you know they really spent a lot of time trying to make it look as, er, as dramatic as possible, you know, the desert and (Yeah) and it really it made a real big effect on the film this situation.

Conal I, I love that scene when he carries her at the end (Yeah) draped in a kind of a white sheet or something (Yeah) and that's such a beautiful image.

Rob But do you think it was over-romantic? I mean ...

 3

Liz Have you seen any good films recently?

Serene Um, yes, I saw *Gladiator* last week.

Liz Is it any good?

Serene I really liked it. It was full of brilliant special effects, it was really dramatic.

Liz Oh, and who was in it?

Serene Well, Russell Crowe was the main gladiator guy, um, and he's quite hot, but he was, he was great, really large stage presence, um, it also had Oliver Reed in it, his last film.

Liz So it was a kind of historical thing?

Serene Yeah, historical, set in the Roman age.

Liz Oh, and what was it about, what was the plot?

Serene Well, it's about, I, I think Russell Crowe starts off as a general, and it's kind of about his fall from grace, but it's obviously not his fault at all, it's all (Oh) just sort of, er, it's all situation, which, which leads to his, this disaster but um, it is, it's really quite exciting. Um, he becomes a gladiator and he has to fight for his life, but because he's such a good fighter he, he becomes a slave, he starts off as a slave and he becomes kind of at the same level as the Caesar.

Liz Really?

Serene Yep.

Liz And what, do you think the acting was good?

Serene Yeah, the acting was very good, I was very impressed. Um, its downfall was probably being a bit too soppy, but ...

Liz Oh, it was really romantic, was it?

Serene It w..., it kind of was, his, his family gets killed, and (Oh no) that's where his passion comes from (Oh) and that kind of brings it down a bit because he goes to heaven and sees them and things, and that's not what you want to see after a big ...

Liz Oh, that's a bit strange, isn't it?

Serene ... dramatic thing, but ...

Liz Oh, so it's romantic, but do you think I'd like it?

Serene Yeah, I think you would because of the, the stage effects are so wonderful and Rome is reconstructed in such a brilliant way. Um, it is quite moving though, and you don't tend to go for the moving type (Yeah) plot.

Liz Oh well, I'll give it a try.

22 WHAT HAVE YOU BEEN UP TO?

 1

Conversation 1

Karen Adam, hello, how are you, I haven't seen you for ages ...

Adam I'm very well, I haven't seen you for a long time either.

Karen Yeah. I suppose you've been busy at work, or ...?

Adam Mm, very busy at work, but mostly I've been, um, I've been, I've been trying to get away from work as often as possible, so, you know, I've done a bit of travelling as well.

Karen Right. Ah, you're always keen on travelling, so where have you been, anywhere interesting?

Adam I went up to, I went up to York last weekend, which was very nice. (Ah, excellent) Very cold, er, and rainy, but er, still, still very pleasant, and, um, I've, I've been sort of planning to do all sorts of trips, sort of um, sort of going through the guidebooks, sort of working out where to go next.

Karen Er, right.

Adam And how about yourself, what have you been up to?

Karen Well, same old thing really. Yeah, doing a lot of work, a lot of overtime, a lot of sort of various bits and pieces really, it seems like, um, time's really gone fast, I can't, can't believe, you know, just bits of this and bits of that.

Conversation 2

Kate So what have you been up to Pam, then?

Pam Well, um, I've just come back from a trip to Madrid, actually.

Kate Oh, right.

Pam I've been there for a few days, um, and I've, I've just, didn't do much really, it was very nice, it was very pleasant, just spending a couple of days.

Kate Holiday?

Pam No, it wasn't a holiday, it was work, but I mean, it's always nice to go to, to somewhere else, um, and I met a few people and went out for meals, and didn't get enough sleep, and that kind of thing. But it was really good. Um, but apart from that, really, I haven't been up to a lot, actually. Not over the last, er, few days or so, few weeks. What about you?

Kate Oh well, I've been, I've been a bit busy with work. I've been on a couple of trips as well.

Pam Uhuh, oh, where did you go?

Kate I went to Spain.

Pam Uhuh.

Kate Little bit of holiday, little bit of work. (Uhum) Um, and, er, I've been a bit busy with the children as well, because, er, we've had, er, birthday party so I've been organizing ...

Pam Oh yes, of course it's ...

Kate ... candles and cakes and presents and so on.

Pam And they both, they both have birthdays about the same time?

Kate Yes, yes, so er, yes things have been a bit hectic.

 3

Conversation 1

A Have you heard that Clare is moving in with that bloke, whatsisname, Myles, the tall one from IT, you know, good-looking, in his forties?

B Um, really? I didn't even know they were seeing each other.

A Nor did I, but apparently they're both into outdoor pursuits, you know, walking, cycling that kind of thing and they got together through a local cycling club.

Conversation 2

A Do you fancy going to the cinema or something tonight?

B Yes, I wouldn't mind. What's on, do you know?

A Er, well, I think that new French film is on at the, what's it called, the, er, Picture Palace.

B Oh yes, I'd like to see that. Any idea what time?

A Er, six thirty, seven-ish? I'm not sure but I'll check in the paper.

Conversation 3

A Erm, I don't suppose you're free on Saturday evening, are you?

B Er, yes I am actually. Why?

A Well, we're having a sort of last minute party and I was wondering if you'd like to come, you know a few drinks, a buffet, things like that.

B Yes, I'd love to. Who else is coming?

A Well, I've invited forty people or so. Er, you'll know most of them I expect.

Conversation 4

A How was the party?

B Um, it was a bit boring actually. All these people with high-flying jobs in the city boasting about how much they earn, all the famous people they know, and so on. (Oh) You know, 'Oh, I've just met so and so', or, um, 'I've just been to New York and done such and such'.

A Yeah, I know what you mean. I hate that kind of party.

[◉ 1]

Michael's story

A Most mountain, most climbers who are really interested in mountaineering, er, always think of the ultimate in mountains, which are the Himalayas, and, er, going on a trip there, but it takes a lot of time and a lot of money to get there. So these things, these sorts of trips are very carefully planned and sometimes they don't come to fruition. But, er, on one occasion when I was in a pub with a friend, he said, 'Shall we go to Nepal, and climb a Himalayan mountain?' and I said 'Yes, why not?' And because he's a very organized sort of bloke, he got it all sorted. And, I was away in Saudi Arabia at the time and so, er, when we when I came back from there it was more or less all organized. And, er, we picked ourselves a trekking peak, which is one which is not too high and therefore too expensive, and which could be done in a month.

B How successful was the actual climb?

A Well, we did what we wanted to do, which was get to the top. Um, we were blessed with very good weather, um, you go, climbing in the Himalaya there are two seasons, and one of them is the November season when, just before the, um, you get the winter storms coming in and, er, but after the, the summer monsoon has finished, and there's a, there's usually a dry steady period of weather but in fact, er, when we got there it was very cold and there'd been a lot of snow, so a lot of the, er, paths and the camp sites which we would have expected to be dry were in fact under snow, which made for a very interesting trip, but not such a comfortable one, and, um, but the main thing was, the weather was steady. It was clear and cold for the whole month we were there. I don't remember any rain at all, um, which, um, made for a physically enjoyable trip.

B With hindsight, would you have done anything differently?

A Well, with hindsight, um, I would have chosen my companions more carefully, but you don't always have, it can be a bit of a luxury and you can't always do that, um, you just have to, um, get together a crowd of people who can afford to go and have the time to go, so that you can actually manage to get the trip done in the first place. And, but our, the team that we got together was, kept changing as people dropped out, so in the end, there was an odd, motley collection of people who didn't really know each other very well and, er, this friend of mine who first suggested it was in fact one of the most difficult people to get on with, especially in a high mountain environment, er, under cold conditions when, er, the weather's lousy, and, er, I think, when we all came back from this trip, this is not untypical, nobody was speaking to anybody, at least I certainly wasn't speaking to anybody else, and we were all glad to get off the plane in London and go our different ways.
On the whole, the whole trip was a, was a great success, and I'm very pleased we went, but I would have liked to have been more involved in the day-to-day running of things, and not been portered and guided all the way because it did leave me with a lot of spare time, and a lot of cold weather, and long dark nights which would have been better spent if I'd had more books. Er, so I would definitely need to take more books next time.
The route itself, um, it was a standard approach route that, er, the easiest way to the mountain, to the top of the mountain but that didn't make it, although it was the easiest way to the top, it wasn't actually that easy. Um, with a bit more time … we could have, um, spent, er, we could have done some exploring, and perhaps found a more interesting way, but I think on the whole, considering it was our first trip, we were quite glad just to be able to get up to the top.

[◉ 2]

Julie's story

A So you're on crutches, why's that?

B Um, yes, bit of a long story really, um, I damaged my knee when I was on my travels, um, last year, and, um, particularly I damaged this knee when I was in Africa and I was climbing Mount Kenya with a friend. And Mount Kenya's a very large mountain, it's five thousand metres, you need three or four days to do it, and, um, … we set off with porters and, um, reached near the summit, er, where we slept the night just below the summit. And it was freezing cold, gets to minus ten, so I was very glad that I had my thermals and my, my four-seasons sleeping bag … um, and the next morning we got up at three o'clock, got to the top of the, the mountain, amazing views, I mean I was just so glad I did it, it was such an achievement and there was snow on the top, and the sun rose, and then very quickly before the ice melted we had to start coming down … and we came down very fast because we were so happy, we were sort of leaping down like goats … um, at our achievement we were really happy … and, um, we walked down all day and got to the place where we were supposed to, um, sleep and, er, there wasn't any room so we were forced basically to keep walking for another day, and so we were, like, coming down the mountain really fast because we needed to get another fifteen kilometres, um, before the sun set … and that was just so much walking coming downhill, going very fast … and, er, I should have remembered, you know, people, people do say you have to take care when you come down a mountain because it's a strain on your knees, and I'd never had a problem with my knees, but, um, … doing all that running down the mountain caused pain in my knees … and I really shouldn't have done it, I should have taken it more slowly, um, and remembered the advice that was given, and, um, another thing that I wish that I'd done was seek medical help um sooner really because I had a pain the next day but it wasn't, for a few days really I kept going on it before I went and got it looked at and now I've got quite an ongoing problem with my knees.

A Oh no, but you're glad you did it?

B Well, I'm glad I did the mountain, but I, I wish I, I wish I'd done it differently.

OXFORD
UNIVERSITY PRESS

Great Clarendon Street, Oxford OX2 6DP

Oxford University Press is a department of the University of Oxford. It furthers the University's objective of excellence in research, scholarship, and education by publishing worldwide in

Oxford New York

Athens Auckland Bangkok Bogotá Buenos Aires Cape Town Chennai Dar es Salaam Delhi Florence Hong Kong Istanbul Karachi Kolkata Kuala Lumpur Madrid Melbourne Mexico City Mumbai Nairobi Paris São Paulo Shanghai Singapore Taipei Tokyo Toronto Warsaw

with associated companies in Berlin Ibadan

Oxford and Oxford English are registered trade marks of Oxford University Press in the UK and in certain other countries

© Oxford University Press 2001

The moral rights of the author have been asserted

Database right Oxford University Press (maker)

First published 2001

ISBN 0-19-434092-9

Designed by Keith Shaw, Threefold Design, Oxford

Printed in Italy by Poligrafico Dehoniano

Acknowledgements

The Author and Publisher are grateful to those who have given permission to reproduce the following extracts and adaptations of copyright material:

p.06 'The mad rush to save time' by Richard Reeves. Appeared in the *Observer* 3 October 1999. © Richard Reeves. Reproduced by permission of the *Observer*.
p.17 'Here's the deal, will you marry me?' by Sharon Krum. Appeared in the *Guardian* 1 July 1999. © Sharon Krum. Reproduced by permission of Sharon Krum.
pp.26, 29, 104, 107, 108 Extracts from Manos Holidays India Brochure October 1995–May 1996. Reproduced

by permission of Panorama and Manos Holidays.
pp.36 & 104 'Will the book be supplanted by electronic technology?' by Simon Waldman and Brian Lang. © the *Guardian* 31 July 1999. Reproduced by permission of the *Guardian*.
p.46 'Boy in 4,500 mile trek to find father' by David Usborne. Appeared in the *Independent* 30 June 1999. Reproduced by permission of Independent Newspapers (UK) Ltd.
p.57 'Under the city's spell' by Lisa Jardine. Appeared in the *Guardian* 22 June 1999. © Lisa Jardine. Reproduced by permission of Lisa Jardine.
p.60 Extracts from *Men Are From Mars, Women Are From Venus* by John Cray. Reproduced by permission of HarperCollins Publishers Ltd.
p.67 'How to complain about goods and services'. Appeared in *Which?* magazine. *Which?* Published by Consumer's Association, 2 Marylebone Road, London NW1 4DF for further information phone 0800 252 100. Reproduced by permission of Consumer's Association.
p.77 Adapted and abridged extracts from *The Future of English?* by David Graddol. Published by The British Council. Reproduced by permission of David Graddol & The British Council.
p.103 'Lonely hearts band together in Berlin, the singles' capital' by Denis Staunton. Appeared in the *Observer* 1 August 1999. © Denis Staunton. Reproduced by permission of the *Observer*.
p.105 'Goodbye to all that?' by Nicci Gerrard. © the *Observer* 31 January 1999. Reproduced by permission of the *Observer*.
pp.106 & 109 Extracts from Phoenix Cinema film listings. Reproduced by permission of Phoenix Cinema, Oxford.
p.107 'How an arranged marriage can work' by Indira Das-Gupta. Appeared in the *Evening Standard* 3 June 1999. Reproduced by permission of Atlantic Syndication Partners.

Although every effort has been made to trace and contact copyright holders before publication, this has not been possible in some cases. We apologize for any apparent infringement of copyright and if notified, the publisher will be pleased to rectify any errors or omissions at the earliest opportunity.

Illustrations by:

Stefan Chabluk p.46; Matthew Cooper pp.20, 68 (television, satellite, etc); Emma Dodd pp.06, 08, 24, 35, 38, 49, 77, 80; Ian Jackson pp.04, 10, 19, 34, 41 (ways of moving), 44, 48, 55, 64, 66, 78; Julian Mosedale pp.12, 16, 22, 23, 37, 41 (tortoise, bull, dog), 60, 63, 65, 68 (snake), 69, 82

Commissioned photography by:

Rob Judges pp.53 (No Stopping sign, One Way sign, speed hump, Park & Ride bus), 73 (Phoenix Picture House)

The Publisher and Authors would like to thank the following for their kind permission to reproduce photographs:

Allsport pp.80 (P.Tournaire/Vandystadt/walking up ridge & at top of pinnacle); Anthony Blake Photo Library pp.11 (M.Brigdale/melon & cake), (S.Irvine/ Sushi), 13 (M.Marque/noodles); Associated Press p.46 (S.Plunkett/Edwin); Bubbles Photo Library pp.11 (C.Rout/girl), 14 (J.Woodcock/student), 43 (C.Rout), 61 (J.Powell/women), 83 (D.Hager/performers); Stuart Conway Photography p.17; Corbis pp.29 (D.Samuel Robbins), 105 (Historical Picture Archive/Piccadilly c.1850), (R.Bird/Frank Lane Picture Agency/harvest), 108 (J.Butchofsky-House/Piccadilly c.1991), (C.George/

horse and cart), (W.Kaehler/camel); GettyOne Stone pp.05 (T.Shonnard), 06 (M.Mathelo/man), (B.Ayres/ woman), (P.Cade/boy), 11 (S.Egan/carrots), 13 (C.Everard), (P.Redman), 14 (D.Bosler/potter), (T.Vine/surgeon), 25 (J.P.Williams/airport), 26 (S.Cohen), 27 (J.& L. Merrill), 28 (S.Outram/island cove), (G.Braasch/rainforest), (H.Grey/friends with video), 30 (S.Kushner/Daniel), (H.Camille/Rashid), (C.Hoehn/Solly), 33 (D.Torckler/dolphin), 36 (J.Tisne/reading book), (S.Cohen/at computer), 39 (I.Burgum/P.Boorman/ laboratory worker), 40 (S.Cohen/party), (E.Grasser/ students on steps), (T.Shonnard/executives), (M.Douet/ supermarket), 46 (R.Ziak/arrest), (J.Ortner/skyscrapers), 50 (J.Pobereskin), (G.Allison/open road), 51 (S.Murphy/ road rage), (N.Giambi/exhaust), 52 (Lineka/cyclists), (G.Allison/wind power), (D.Woodfall/recycling), 53 (K.Biggs/aerial view), (E.Pritchard/tram), 54 (S.Cohen/bowling), (D.Waugh/Bath), 56 (R.Estakhrian/ tower blocks), (J.Hawkes/semi-detatched houses), (J.Lawrence/cottage), 57 (P.Cade), 58 (C.Raw/fields), (R.Talbot/mountains), (J.Chard/desert), 59 (B.De Hogues/Paris), (C.Waite/cliffs), 61 (A.Thornton/road rage), 62 (R.E.Daemmrich/parent), 64 (W.Sallaz/plane), 73 (R.Etkin/projector), (A.Marsh/popcorn), (J.Cotier/ clapperboard), (S.Austin Welch/seats), 74 (S.McClymont), 76 (P.Chesley/air traffic control), (O.Strewe/stock market), (L.Beziat/man at computer), 79 (K.Su), 83 (E.Grasser/party), (Fisher/Thatcher/ speech); Ronald Grant Archive p.70 (© 1998 Polygram Filmed Entertainment ñ All Rights Reserved/Notting Hill); Impact Photo Library pp.14 (M.Black/dustmen), 30 (A.Johnstone/prison door); Katz Pictures pp.30 (D.Modell/man in room), 31 (R.Baker/boys playing), 39 (R.Baker/IPG/soldiers training), (Peterson/Saba-Rea/boy looking at guns), 46 (S.Attal/roller-blading), 62 (T.Stoddart/IPG/soldier); NHPA p.81 (J.Warwick/Mount Kenya), (A.N.T./Mount Everest); Photofusion pp.31 (P.Baldesare/phone booth), (R.Smith/stairway with graffiti), 33 (R.Eaton/housing), 39 (M.Campbell/nose-rings etc); Pictorial Press p.70 (Easy Rider), (JAAP Buitendijk © 2000 Universal Studios/Gladiator), (Miramax International/Emma), (Paramount/Rear Window), (Laurel & Hardy); Picture Colour Library p.25 (train), 28 (temple), 56 (mansion flats); Powerstock Zefa pp.105 (woman and trolley), (cyclists), 108 (deck chair); Frank Spooner Pictures p.21 (A.Berg); Stock Shot pp.64 (D.Willis/camper), 80 (H.Taylor/crossing crevasse), 83 (J.Stock/expedition)

The Publisher and Author would like to thank the following teachers and readers for their invaluable help with the development of the manuscript:

Maggie Baigent; Theresa Clementson; Jo Cooke; Jane Hudson; Lynne White; Jo Savage and Simon Wilkinson and the staff and students at the Bell School, Budapest; the staff and students at International House, Budapest; the staff and students at the British Council, Bologna and Valencia.

The Author would like to thank everyone who has helped with the writing of this book, especially Ian Thompson for his advice on the treatment of articles, Stuart Jeffrey for his help with setting up the interviews in lesson 09, and all the people too numerous to mention who gave up their time to be interviewed and recorded.